THE
NETWORKING
SURVIVAL GUIDE

Andrew -

Happy networkj!

Diane

THE
NETWORKING
SURVIVAL GUIDE

Practical Advice to Help You Gain Confidence, Approach People, and Get the Success You Want

SECOND EDITION

DIANE DARLING

New York   Chicago   San Francisco   Lisbon   London   Madrid   Mexico City
Milan   New Delhi   San Juan   Seoul   Singapore   Sydney   Toronto

The McGraw·Hill Companies

Copyright © 2010, 2003 by Diane C. Darling. All rights reserved. Printed in the United States of America. Except as permitted under the United States Copyright Act of 1976, no part of this publication may be reproduced or distributed in any form or by any means, or stored in a data base or retrieval system, without the prior written permission of the publisher.

1 2 3 4 5 6 7 8 9 0   DOC/DOC   1 5 4 3 2 1 0

ISBN   978-0-07-171758-8
MHID   0-07-171758-7

This publication is designed to provide accurate and authoritative information in regard to the subject matter covered. It is sold with the understanding that the publisher is not engaged in rendering legal, accounting, or other professional service. If legal advice or other expert assistance is required, the services of a competent professional person should be sought.

> —*From a Declaration of Principles jointly adopted by a Committee of the American Bar Association and a Committee of Publishers*

McGraw-Hill books are available at special quantity discounts to use as premiums and sales promotions, or for use in corporate training programs. To contact a representative please e-mail us at bulksales@mcgraw-hill.com.

Library of Congress Cataloging-in-Publication Data

Darling, Diane.
   The networking survival guide : practical advice to help you gain confidence, approach people, and get the success you want / Diane C. Darling. — Completely updated 2nd ed.
     p. cm.
Includes bibliographical references and index.
   ISBN-13: 978-0-07-171758-8
   ISBN-10: 0-07-171758-7
   1. Career development   2. Business networks.   3. Social networks.
I. Title
   HF5381.D26 2010
   650.1'3—dc22   2009052620

To Mom—I miss you more than ever!

Contents

Acknowledgments

It's hard to believe that when I first wrote *The Networking Survival Guide, social networking* wasn't a term, *friend* wasn't a verb, and if someone asked for your Twitter handle, you'd be quite puzzled.

All that has changed significantly in less than 10 years. I'm often asked whether face-to-face networking will become extinct. My sense is that online networking will help to facilitate face-to-face and vice versa. There are mistakes we make, both in person and online. But at the end of the day, we all need others to get things done.

This book wouldn't exist without networking. Thank you to Martha Donovan, who told JoAnn Lublin at the *Wall Street Journal* about my workshops. And it was in that paper on December 4, 2001, that an acquisitions editor at McGraw-Hill read the story and called with a question that I never thought I'd hear: "Would you like to write a book?"

I am also often asked who is better at networking—men or women. I believe the differences aren't identified by gender. You are either smart or . . . well, "stupid" seems harsh. But if you have a good network in place, when you need something, you have people to call.

As always, it takes a village to write a book. There are many to thank.

The crew at McGraw-Hill, who gave me freedom, trust, and feedback.

Thank you to Todd Randolph for his significant contribution to writing and editing. His clarity and fresh perspective kept me focused and reassured.

To the many introverts who have inspired me and helped me to be more comfortable in my own skin. I do like people, I really do! But sometimes they just wear me out. I now understand the difference between friendly and extroverted.

To the many newsletter subscribers who share their stories and insights, thank you! I wish I could meet each and every one of you. Please keep your stories coming.

Introduction

Congratulations—you've just made an investment in your life. While we may enjoy the fantasy that we can do everything ourselves, it's just not realistic. We need other people. But how do we build and maintain relationships? How do we decide how much time to spend networking? What mistakes should we avoid?

Throughout this book are stories and examples of how people have used networking—both online and off. These will give you insights into and ideas about how to make connections. You will have an opportunity to hear these people's experiences firsthand.

There are exercises that I encourage you to do. Find a partner or group and practice some of the tips that I provide. If you are an introvert, find a networking buddy to go to events with you. If you are an extrovert, try to do some active listening.

You will also learn of the many ways to network that you may overlook. Here are a few examples:

- Writing an article, blog, or book
- Speaking
- Connecting people to each other
- Asking a question at an event

- Being on a panel
- Serving on a committee
- Sending a thank-you note
- Making a referral
- Participating online, be it social networking sites or online groups or communities

Most important, just get started. Whether you are beginning your career, looking to advance, or even finding ways to retire, other people are your best resource for getting anything accomplished in a cost-effective, time-efficient way.

Even outside of work, we associate with people that we like and get to know—often through friends or friends of friends. Think about your last vacation or restaurant experience. We frequently learn about opportunities through word of mouth.

As you read the book, I encourage you to keep a list of people who come to mind. Maybe they are former neighbors, colleagues, or classmates. You may be able to find them online. Create an e-mail to send to them. Use this book as a great way to reconnect.

Here's a sample:

Dear _____,

I'm reading a book about networking called *The Networking Survival Guide*, and I realize it's been a while since we were in touch. It's so easy to get busy with life, and I wanted to hear what's new with you.

I remember _____ (include a story or remembrance) at work, school, in the neighborhood.

For me, life has been both good and challenging. (Fill in a few stories or updates.)

I look forward to hearing about you.

Best regards,

Preferably we stay in touch and don't contact people *only* when we need something. Use this book as a reason to reach out and make connections. Then when you need something, you will already be on these people's radar.

Without a doubt, the hardest thing I ever do is ask others for help. I feel as if I've failed or as if I'm inadequate whenever I do. I'm almost always wrong. I'm learning (mind you, it's taken some time) that others do like and want to help. In many cases, they have skills and talents that I don't, and the problem is resolved quickly and efficiently.

I've created a Web site (www.EffectiveNetworking.com/Resources) with extra resources if you are interested in creating a book group to do these exercises and help one another. Or just do them on your own. If you have tips or techniques you would like to share, please do so. I can't promise that I'll be able to answer each e-mail, but please send your thoughts.

Be good to yourself and invite others to be in your network. Please keep me posted!

I look forward to seeing what happens next.

Happy networking!

Diane Darling

How to contact Diane:

E-mail: Diane@EffectiveNetworking.com

Phone: 617.247.2700

(Please note due to the volume of inquiries, I often am not able to respond to each person individually.)

For updates and random newsletters, please subscribe to my newsletter on www.EffectiveNetworking.com.

1

Overview

Getting to know you
Getting to know all about you
Getting to like you
Getting to hope you like me
      ~ From *The King and I*, Rogers and Hammerstein

Paula Boggs loved cookies. So when the executive assistant to the CEO called to tell her that cookies had been delivered for her, she said she would be right over.

She was very excited about her new job as the general counsel for Starbucks. She opened the card, and the gift was from Doc Spade. He was the mail guy who came around each day at the law firm of Perkins Elmer and Ellis, where she had previously worked. Paula had always enjoyed her conversations with him. Their chats were a welcome diversion from her cases, and he was a nice guy to catch up with on what was happening in his life and at the firm. She thought it curious that Doc would send her a congratulatory gift on her new position, and even more that it should come via the CEO's office. The executive assistant explained. Jim Donald, the president and CEO of

Starbucks, was from the same small town south of Seattle as Doc. When he saw that someone from Perkins was a candidate for the general counsel's job, Jim called to get a reference from his friend of 40 years—Doc Spade.

It is indeed crucial to keep your network up-to-date and refreshed. Having said that, there are many people that we overlook because we assume that they do not have anything to offer. Fortunately for Paula, she realized that anyone and everyone was worthy of her time and appreciation.

Maybe I'm just lazy, but one of the reasons that I like networking is that others help me. There's just no way I can get everything done by myself. If I ask people to make an introduction or give me an idea, it means that more minds are better than one.

From your first conversation in the morning until your last conversation at night, you are networking. Many people don't realize that they are networking when that is exactly what they are doing. If you have lunch with someone a few times a year to stay in touch, that's networking. If you participate on a board or community group, you are networking. If you recommend an attorney to your neighbor, you are networking.

- Have you ever recommended someone for a job?
- How did you get your biggest client?
- Is there someone you meet every so often for a cup of coffee?
- How did you find out about your favorite restaurant?
- How did you find that great vacation spot?
- Where did you find out about your apartment or house?
- Whom do you call to raise money for your favorite charity?

Networking is the art of building and sustaining mutually beneficial relationships. There is a worthwhile reason for all parties to participate. It happens at home, at work, in our community, with everyone.

THERE ARE THREE TYPES OF PEOPLE—WHICH ONE ARE YOU?

It is said that there are three types of people in the world:

1. Those who make it happen
2. Those who watch it happen
3. Those who wonder what happened

Think of an inverted stoplight—do you make things go, do you proceed with caution, or do find yourself stopped dead in your tracks? Networked people make things happen, and they know others who do so as well. They are sought after as problem solvers and solution providers.

Which light are you? In this book, we'll discuss how you can make things happen and teach yourself the networking tools and techniques that will make you successful.

WHY READ THIS BOOK?

I taught my first networking workshop to a nonprofit association that wanted to offer its members some tools and techniques to maximize their networking opportunities. While networking opportunities abound, the process isn't clear and is open to interpretation. That can cause some confusion and frustration. *The Networking Survival Guide* is designed to help make order out of chaos. It focuses on two facets of networking:

1. The outside, the practical, the skills, or the "how-to." These are aspects that can easily be learned with some training and practice.

2. The inside, spiritual education. This is the connection to others that we feel when we network and the possible reasons we may be hesitant to do so.

Here are some comments and questions that I kept hearing. See if they resonate with you.

- When I meet someone, I don't know what to say.
- I feel as if I'm bothering people.
- If someone doesn't return my call in a week, do I call again?
- When I'm given someone's name, is it okay to use it?
- How often should I follow up?
- What method is best?
- How many times should I follow up?
- What organizations should I be a part of?
- Networking takes too much time.

Be easy on yourself. So far, it's been the luck of your family, your education, your genes, and your environment that has determined your networking aptitude. Somehow you were expected to learn this essential lifelong skill from a variety of people and places without a curriculum or any structure.

Imagine about five or six people who all wear the same size shoe. They take off their right shoe, move one place to the right, and put on the right shoe of the person standing next to them. I bet the shoe feels a bit weird.

That is what this book will do for you and networking. You are going to learn and/or refine best practices and adapt them to your needs. Best practices are like new shoes: The more you wear them, the more they become made just for you. They protect what literally holds you up, they express your individuality, and they anchor you.

Summary: Getting to know people and letting others get to know you begins the cycle that empowers the networking process. Best practices make you feel confident, like your favorite shoes.

REASONS WE NETWORK

No man is an island, entire of itself; every man is a piece of the continent, a part of the main.

~ JOHN DONNE (1572–1631)

You need other people in your life, and they need you. It is unrealistic and impractical to do everything by yourself. You need others to help you get things done, both in business and personally. Why should someone help? Why are you asking?

When you know the right person to get a task accomplished, and that person returns your phone call, you save

- Time
- Money
- Energy

Some of the common reasons that people network are

- Business development or sales
- Raising business capital
- Professional/career development
- Getting a job, assistance with career management, or a job transition
- Recruiting board members, management, or employees
- Fund-raising for a nonprofit, such as a charity or an educational institution
- Social or personal reasons

When I first wrote *The Networking Survival Guide* in 2003, *friend* was a noun, not a verb. A lot has changed in these past few years. Social networking sites have given the average person access to many people who would otherwise be out of reach.

That's both good and bad. In this revised edition, I'll share with you the best ways to intertwine offline and online networking. I'll introduce you to a concept that I call "hybrid" networking, which is a blend of the two.

In the past, our business and personal networks were separated. The term *social networking* just meant going to a barbecue or some other place where you were unlikely to see people you knew from work.

This book is written from a business perspective, but the principles are also applicable to social or personal networking. Most of the examples will involve professionals who are seeking to expand their network. For example, suppose you want to start a business, and you need working capital. You want to meet people who can help you. If you are job hunting, you want to expand your network to learn about companies and where you can make a contribution. If you are raising funds for a music camp, you want to find alumni and/or music lovers who will be more likely to make a donation.

Whatever your reasons for networking, *The Networking Survival Guide* will help you determine the most effective techniques for your situation. Who is the best person to approach? What do you need to know? What is the best method? What are some strategies that will help you succeed?

When you get directions to someone's house, there are typically several ways to get to the destination. If there is construction, the path may change. Similarly, in networking, there are many ways for you to arrive at your destination. The goal is to find a path that works for you. On occasion, try a new route.

Summary: Whatever your reason for networking, it is a valuable lifelong skill. Get started, learn, and have fun!

NETWORKING CAN BE LEARNED

Often I hear people say that they can't network—they just are not wired that way. My goal is to show you that even the most introverted person can indeed network. I won't try to make you be someone you are not. And you absolutely don't have to *love* walking into a cocktail party. I do want to share with you ways in which you can make connections—both online and off—that are rewarding and comfortable.

Every successful professional realizes at some point that he needs business training in order to reach the next level of his career. It is at this point that we begin to understand that we cannot do everything ourselves, and that indeed there may be some skills that we need to develop.

When our company, Effective Networking, Inc., leads a workshop, typically people are a bit nervous at the beginning. They know that they are going to be doing things that are outside of their present comfort zone, such as introducing themselves to the group, doing some role playing, and learning new skills.

During a workshop, my first question often is, "Who loves to floss?" The facial expressions say it all. They glance at the door and wonder how they can slip out. Often there are one or two oral hygiene fanatics who raise their hand and say that they love to floss. Next I ask, "Who is competent at flossing?" Ah—the shoulders go down and the smiles appear.

Your dentist doesn't really care if you floss. They're *your* teeth, not your dentist's! But if you want to keep them, it's best to take care of them, even if flossing is a chore you really don't like. It's okay not to *like* it; you just have to be competent at it.

Lastly, I ask, "Who outsources flossing?" Usually that gets a laugh. I then point out that you can't outsource networking, either. So you might as well learn to do it well.

Give yourself permission to learn networking and do it well, even if you don't love it. It's one of those skills—like typing—that you'll be really glad you took the time to get right.

Networking is like the express (HOV) lane on the highway. It works in a crowd, it requires more than one person, and it gets you where you want to get a lot faster!

Those who are intellectually gifted value "people" skills and know that these skills will help them get things done in life and accomplish the task more easily, more quickly, and with less hassle to all around them.

Summary: Be a lifelong learner and add networking to your portfolio of talents.

BENJAMIN FRANKLIN AND THE INTERNET

Each generation must transform the knowledge of the past into the promise of the future.

       ~ UNKNOWN

In 1727, Benjamin Franklin and other patriots formed a club for the purpose of "mutual improvement." The group valued education so highly that the club members were instrumental in starting the University of Pennsylvania. In his autobiography, Franklin writes, "I had form'd most of my genius acquaintance into a club for mutual improvement, we met on Friday evenings."[1]

Some of the questions required for membership were

- Do you sincerely declare that you love mankind in general, of whatever profession or religion?
- Do you love truth for truth's sake, and will you endeavour impartially to find and receive it yourself, and communicate it to others?[2]

Imagine what it would be like to meet each week with people of the caliber of Benjamin Franklin. The value of their intellects and viewpoints was so high that they wanted to learn from one another and share their knowledge.

In the 1700s, this group was obviously limited to those in the geographic area. We are now blessed with access to the entire world via the Internet. You can learn from others who are many miles away, and vice versa. The talent pool available to you has grown from your local neighborhood to a global one.

At first, many of those who embraced the Internet assumed that it would replace face-to-face interaction. While the Internet has facilitated communication in many regards, in-person time is still highly valued. When the economy shifted, the people who were able to survive and even thrive were the people who had a network in place and knew how to call upon it.

We are indeed blessed at this time to have *both* technology and face-to-face interaction as part of our networking repertoire. In this book, you'll learn how to create your own "club of mutual improvement" and find ways to maximize your use of technology to enhance and manage your network for life.

Summary: We all want to belong. Find a group of people that share your interests and where you can be successful.

THE "PRESENT"

Yesterday's the past and tomorrow's the future. Today is a gift—which is why they call it the present.

~ BILL KEANE

The word *present* is extremely important in networking. It has multiple meanings, and all of them are relevant to networking.

- To be successful in networking, you need to be *present*. You need to be in attendance. Some people say that they can multitask, but when they are challenged, many of these people retreat and admit that none of the projects (or people) that they are dealing with are getting the attention they deserve. If you are speaking with someone in person, she is your priority. If this isn't the case, then cancel the meeting, because you really aren't present. You are preoccupied.

- "My *present* information tells me that the outlook for next year is very strong." Your information is current. It is relative. It should be listened to by others. Be a news junkie!

- "I'd like to *present* the Ambassador of Spain." *Present* can also mean an introduction. You are facilitating a meeting between two people.

- Pre-sent—before you can be present, you need to do your preparation work. Then you can genuinely be present because you are familiar with the audience, organization, and so on. *Pre* means "before." Before you send yourself, know where you are going.

- Last but certainly not least, remember that the word *present* also means gift. When you are networking, you are a gift to that person, and he is a gift to you! By solving the person's problem, you take away his frustration and give him peace. You are a solution to the person's problem, and perhaps vice versa.

Summary: In order for networking to be worthwhile, you need to give as much as you take.

WHY THE OTHER PERSON SHOULD CARE

No person was ever honored for what he received. Honor has been the reward for what he gave.

~ CALVIN COOLIDGE

Everyone in the entire world listens to the same radio station: WII-FM—"what's in it for me"! You make time for others and they make time for you when there is some benefit for both parties. The payback doesn't have to be tangible; in fact, in many cases, it is not. When you take the time to learn about someone else's livelihood and interests, you are more likely to get that person's time and attention.

If it's not clear what's in it for the other person, then acknowledge that. Say, "I'm not sure what I can do for you; however, I want you to know that I appreciate your efforts and hope you will let me know how I can help you."

People do not always expect cash compensation or immediate remuneration. In some cases, it's getting to know you and having someone appreciate your skills that merit a person's effort.

Listen to the challenges that the other person is facing. When I was seeking funding to grow my business, I spoke with someone who could help. In the course of the conversation, she mentioned that she was looking for a contact at a specific organization in Dallas. I introduced her to someone who had connections there, and she was thrilled. I had called to get help from her and ended up giving help instead.

Summary: You have something to give everyone. It just takes a few questions to figure it out. If it's not immediately apparent, then stay connected to people of the quality that you want in your life. Something good will come of it.

PERSONAL BRAND

Wherever you go, you represent more than just yourself. Years ago, when I was working in Europe, I had a colleague in the travel industry who commented on how difficult it must be for me to be an American. She explained that from her perspective, the world looks to the United States to fix global problems and blames the United States when things go wrong. She was delighted to be from a smaller country, so that when people met her, they didn't expect so much from her country, and, indirectly, from her.

Companies create brands for each of their products. The messages associated with these brands convey to us reliability, value, and trust. We feel safe with brands we have known for years—for example, Ivory soap's claim of being 99.44 percent pure.

When you see someone walking down the street with a Starbucks cup, you automatically make assumptions about that person. It's the same with someone wearing Nike shoes or driving a VW bug. Brand is a combination of function and emotion. The product or service has to meet our needs, but we also have to like it.

What builds or destroys a brand is its *consistency*. It's frustrating if the product or service sometimes works and sometimes doesn't. Imagine what it would be like if your smartphone or PDA decided to synchronize some of the data, but not quite all. After a while, you wouldn't trust the product. The same is true with people. Inconsistent or unpredictable behavior is a quick killer of anyone's professional or personal success.

People have a brand, too. It's called their "reputation." Are you known as someone who gets things done? What do people say about how you work with others? Do you have a strong and accessible network? How do others perceive your temperament? These are things that people decide after they have met you and worked with you.

Your message to others starts much earlier. The way you dress, walk, wear your hair, and speak; whom you hang out with—all this affects your personal brand. If you are sincere, on time, and funny, then others get a positive feeling about you. It enhances your brand. If you are late, are sarcastic, or interrupt, those you are dealing with will feel disrespected.

When you are on the phone, you are creating an image for the other person. Can she hear you typing? Are you distracted during the call? Do you speak clearly? Does your voice go up, making you sound like a teenager, or as if you don't know what you are talking about, or as if maybe you are Canadian. Eh?

When you are online, the same is true. Someone takes a look at your LinkedIn profile or Facebook page and makes a decision about whether or not to move forward with the communication. Don't sabotage yourself and "overshare" online. On the other hand, don't be afraid to reflect some personality. Our trust in others increases as we feel we know them better. Social networking sites allow that to happen more quickly than in the past.

Sometimes people complain about the amount of information that is available online and that it can create an inaccurate image of them. Here are my two responses. First, before there was Google, there was gossip! People have been talking about you behind your back for centuries. You just didn't know it. Second, you have far more control over what information is shared about you online than was ever possible when the town busybody set to work!

How much time do you have to make a first impression? It might be as little as 3 seconds or as much as 20. What can you do in that time to create a positive personal brand? Brenda Smith is the managing partner of Prophet, a firm that helps clients manage their brands as a strategic asset. Her suggestions include the following:

- Recognize your personal strengths and gifts.
- Think about how you connect best with people.
- Consider what your target audience needs and wants.
- Identify the value you deliver to meet those needs and wants.

- Communicate in a way that reaches your constituents in their hearts and minds via the channels that work best for you and for them.
- Recognize the gaps in your personal brand.
- Invest time and energy to overcome those gaps.

Whew! That's a lot to cover in way under a minute. The first two points address *how* you will make the impression. Especially in a business context, the way people perceive you when you meet affects their perception long after the first meeting. Being something other than who you are will make you seem artificial and set an awkward tone for future interaction. You have something unique to share— yourself! Relax and go with it.

The next two relate to *what* you want to communicate. Introducing yourself should be about more than your name. It is your best opportunity to present yourself as a solution. The remaining points are longer-term, strategic methods to develop better relationships.

After you have created that first impression, what are you doing with it? Do you build on it or let it fade away? A good first impression is an invitation to advance the relationship. Later in the book, I will talk more about best practices for strengthening the relationships you are learning to create.

As noted earlier, the first impression is the introduction of your personal brand to that individual or group. However, it's always helpful for a new brand to receive some advance promotion. In networking, this can come in the form of a referral or simply one's reputation. When we purchase a product or service, we are more willing to select it if we or someone we know has had a good experience with it in the past. When it meets or exceeds our expectations, we feel empowered and enthusiastic about recommending it to others. A personal brand can act the same way for an individual.

What are the results when you have a successful brand?

- You have improved self-confidence.
- You are in demand.
- You help others succeed.
- You know how you are different from your competitors.

Your brand also affects the bigger picture. When people meet you, they immediately put you in the same category as all the other people they have met in the past who are in the same group you are. That may be based on appearance, gender, profession (e.g., as Shakespeare put it, "let's kill all the lawyers"), country of origin, the company you work for, and much more. There isn't anything you can do about this, but you should be aware that it exists. If you had a bad experience at a certain store, that company's name remains blacklisted in your mind. If you meet someone who works for that company, you immediately think of this negative experience.

If you work for a company, remember that your behavior reflects on it as well as on you. Every day I walk through a complex in Boston that includes a Sheraton hotel. One time when I was walking in, I saw the bellman shaking his head as he looked into a taxi. As I got closer, I realized what was going on: the taxi driver was holding a $20 bill and trying to bribe the bellman to give his cab the next fare.

The bellman's decision not to accept the bribe and to give the fare to the next taxi made a statement about him, his company (Sheraton), bellmen, Bostonians, and men too!

Summary: Your conduct reflects on you and everyone in your life. Have respect for yourself and others whom you care about and who care about you.

YOU ARE A CEO

Every person who is reading this book is a chief executive officer (CEO). Each day you make the same decisions a CEO does. You determine where your money goes, you run interference when there is a dispute, you create short-term and long-term strategy, you add to your team (find a mate and/or have children), you relocate, and you decide where you want to go in life and how to get there. Even if you feel that you are not involved in making any decisions, you are choosing not to get involved. That's an executive decision on your part.

The CEO is the leader of a company, and you are the leader of your life. You make decisions about what to do and what not to do. As your skills develop, you can apply the same principles to networking. An executive's primary job is being the face of the company. You need to do that for You, Inc. Find opportunities, take calculated risks, and create a great team to help you get things done.

Summary: When a challenge presents itself, don't shy away from it. Take it as an opportunity to practice your CEO skills.

Business and Social Networking: "Affinitas ex Machina," or "Connections Via the Machine"

David Flint, founder of TechVenue.com, has a fascinating perspective on social networking that I asked him to share.

The business and social networking playing field is very crowded and can at times feel like an exercise in following the rabbit hole down as far as it goes, with all of the choices and features swirling around our heads in the Web 2.0 world and beyond. One thing I've learned that helps narrow things down is: "know thyself." I say this not only personally, but also in how you present yourself to the world. Individually and as part of your company, you are your own "brand," and you deserve to have a clear differentiation. Then you can better identify the online and offline audiences that you wish to participate with and the value proposition that you bring to them. Start by rediscovering these "Webations" about yourself:

Identification: Who is your audience?
Orientation: What are your present angle and your future direction?

Classification: Are you in a certain vertical market, age, vocation, or interest area?

"Funification": How "fun" and easy are you to communicate with, your service to use, events you host or frequent?

Diane has already done a wonderful job in explaining what the purpose of networks and networking is, what it is and is not. One key aspect of converting online connections into real-world connections and even successful events is that, once you have defined your relationships to your audience as described in this chapter, you consider one main strategy that moviemakers use to draw people to the theaters: trailers.

A 15-second elevator pitch is not enough anymore to garner lasting interest, let alone develop a relationship. What's the point? You are your own "screenplay." Take a cue from moviemakers and develop your own "trailer" to attract, inform, engage, and persuade people to use your services or events. Now, I'm not saying that everyone should literally make a YouTube video right away and throw it up there to see if it sticks. Rather, first you must really "be" the trailer you portray and be consistent with it, whatever the medium you choose to use.

I recently read the book *Screenwriting: The Art, Craft, and Business of Film and Television Writing*, by Richard Walter, professor and screenwriting faculty chairman at UCLA. What I learned I was able to translate over to networking. Overall, online networking and converting online to offline activities (events, business transactions, and so on) is akin to designing and producing a screenplay. It's your storyboard action (online presence, ads) that motivates real live actors and audiences (clients, event attendees) to relate to your offerings.

Online networking can help play the part of the storyboard and/or "movie trailer" so that people can get a taste of how fulfilling the "whole enchilada" will be. Like it or not, whether you're a businessperson engaging in a transaction or an event producer at any level, you are a producer and director—you are producing something real from something that is communicated virtually and connecting the dots in between to the real world. Start creating your own blockbuster today!

"Lights—Camera—Action!"

2

What Networking Is and What It Isn't

Networks exist to foster self-help, to exchange information, to change society, improve productivity and work life, and to share resources. They are structured to transmit information in a way that is quicker, more high touch, and more energy-efficient than any other process we know.
~ JOHN NAISBITT, *Megatrends*

Many people think of networking as involving dreary cocktail parties and strangers pushing business cards at them. I know I used to. Then I realized that a lot of things I do every day are all forms of networking:

- Referring someone who is looking for an apartment to a landlord
- Suggesting a restaurant to a work colleague
- Picking up someone's mail for her while she's on vacation
- Answering someone's e-mail

- Returning someone's call
- Letting someone know that you are sick and need someone to bring chicken soup
- Joining a nonprofit board

According to Merriam-Webster, *networking* as a verb did not even exist until 1966. One can hypothesize that a network of people was not as necessary prior to that date, since people rarely moved from their home community. Given that we had known most of the people in that community for our entire lives, there was less to discover, as relationships were handed down from generation to generation. Today nearly 20 percent of Americans move each year. Creating a new network in an unfamiliar community can be taxing. The need to find a new school, dry cleaner, plumber, and other services can be exhausting. Not to mention just learning how to get from one place to another. It's no surprise that cars with a built-in GPS system are selling fast.

New relationships must be formed each time we relocate, and doing that is a lot of work. Anyone who has ever moved knows that you don't just pick up the phone book and pick a school. You ask others to help you. Thus, when you network, it reduces the stress of an already taxing situation.

Although Woody Allen says, "80 percent of life is showing up," it's important to remember the other 20 percent. You have to do something when you arrive.

Networking is an *activity*. That's the *ing* part of the word. It requires your participation. Our network is the group of people who want us to be safe and secure—personally and professionally. It is those who are willing to lend a hand, share an idea, champion our efforts, and, when appropriate, challenge us to reach new heights.

Networking is

- Sharing knowledge and contacts
- Helping others

- Building relationships *before* you need them
- Getting the help *you* need when you need it
- Getting more done with less effort

Most important, remember, networking is a skill that anyone can learn!

I've talked about what networking is. Let's review what it is *not*, so that there isn't any confusion. Networking is not:

- Selling anything
- Asking for a job
- Soliciting a donation
- Securing funding

Summary: Networking is building relationships before you need them! Then when you need them, you know whom to call, and they will want to help you.

MARKETING, NETWORKING, AND SELLING—WHAT'S THE DIFFERENCE?

Marketing, networking, and selling are interdependent, like the beef, mushrooms, and red wine in a *boeuf bourgignon*. The three components are more powerful together than apart. I use the term *selling* to describe any situation in which someone is asking for something, even if it is a nonprofit organization, a contact within your company, or a job interview. When you ask for a donation to your university or your cause, you are to a certain extent selling. The job hunter who lands the job sold her skills better than other candidates for the position.

Let's come up with some descriptions so that we understand what these activities are. (See Figure 2-1.)

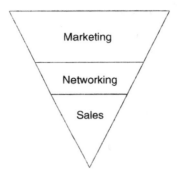

Figure 2-1 Marketing, Networking, and Sales

- *Marketing* gets things started. It is an integrated promotional campaign that includes Web sites, advertising, public relations, and brochures designed to create awareness of your product or service. Marketing casts a wide net, educates a target audience, and creates awareness.
- *Networking* is the next step; it narrows the scope. It is people-driven, not company- or media-driven. It's personal. It connects people who do things or solve problems for each other. Networking is cost-effective.
- *Sales* defines the relationship between the party with the need and the one that can meet that need. Essentially, sales says what each party will do in the transaction. It is far easier to arrive at this happy point with good networking, and the sales process itself is much easier when marketing has set expectations appropriately.

It is tempting to skip the networking piece and go for the sale. Anxious job hunters, for example, want to get their applications in as quickly as possible to beat the rush. However, being the first résumé on the hiring manager's desk is much less compelling than being referred by someone whom that manager knows and trusts. Taking the time to investigate the opportunity and see if there is anyone you know that might be connected to the company or the individual is well worth a slight delay in putting in your application. The same rules apply to the salesperson targeting a new account or the nonprofit seeking large donations.

Think about it this way: how many people do you know who have attended a networking event and walked out with a signed contract for business? Or walked out with a signed job offer, benefits negotiated, and references checked? (Assuming that you wanted to work for that person sight unseen!)

Most of us would be properly wary if those "too good to be true" situations happened. It's unwise to put the cart before the horse. The cart is likely to go astray, and the attached horse will get dragged along with it.

When we want to purchase something, we gather enough information so that we can make our decision, take action, and then move on. Today, with the wealth of information that is available online, buyers can easily access information that used to be available exclusively from the salesperson. By the time we get to the "buy" stage, we have conducted due diligence and determined that we have enough information to make a proper decision. Networking is valuable to the purchaser in accessing information, and to the seller in understanding more about the buyer's needs.

Summary: It is tempting to rush through the process. Be patient.

NETWORKING VERSUS SCHMOOZING

You schmooze, you lose.
> ~ LENI CHAUVIN, founder of Superstar Networking

Networking is sometimes dismissed as "schmoozing." Schmoozing has the connotation of creating a very superficial connection that benefits only the schmoozer. It's a take situation.

Going back to the dictionary, there are several definitions of schmoozing and how it is about casual conversation. There is also a definition, "to gain an advantage or make a social connection." That's how most people feel when someone is schmoozing them. We don't want to be schmoozed or (even worse) be categorized as a schmoozer!

Conferences, trade shows, and other meetings often have "networking" time. I've never seen it advertised as "schmooze" time.

One of the biggest pet peeves I hear from people is that people want something from them without even a *thought* of giving back. After a while, this can be quite frustrating and can wear out an otherwise good relationship. We can all probably think of one or two people that we rarely hear from unless they want something from us.

Networking, on the other hand, is an ongoing relationship based on mutual benefit. The benefit does not need to be constant, but establishing and maintaining the relationship ensures that when a need arises, the connection is there. Those who are uncomfortable with the idea of networking should think of it as an investment—one that will yield dividends over time. Nobody ever confused schmoozing with investing!

We have different people in our lives for different reasons. Some of them help us to make money, some make us laugh, and others stretch our minds. With some we share a hobby or an interest. Many we just like. A few we don't like, and they probably aren't crazy about us either.

Time is limited, and we need to make difficult choices. Whom do we make time for? Who makes time for us? Why?

The simple answer is:

• We make time for people whom we like and who like us.

- We find time for people who make us feel positive, energized, and worthy.
- We take time for people to whom we can offer value and from whom we can derive benefits.

What do we do with the rest? They belong in our "acquaintance" network. They are not to be brushed off completely—remember the saying about burning bridges!—but they do not merit the time and energy needed to cultivate them as active networking contacts.

What creates that chemistry for the three categories just given? What connects us? What can we do to attract positive and energetic people? What can we do to be one of those people? Simply reverse roles. What approach do you respond to? Why do you make time for some people and not others? You have the answers right now.

Summary: Be sincere and give back.

TYPES OF NETWORKING

In a nutshell, networking falls into two categories:

- ***Strategic.*** This is planned. There is a specific person that you want to meet for a specific reason. You ask mutual acquaintances for an introduction.
- ***Serendipitous.*** This is an unplanned or chance encounter that leads to a mutually beneficial relationship.

In *The Networking Survival Guide*, we'll discuss both; however, the focus will be on strategic networking. Why? Strategic networking has a stated purpose and therefore a desired outcome. By definition, there are results that we want and consequences if those results do not materialize. We have in our mind what will go right, and also what could go wrong. We anticipate every sentence, body movement, action, and reaction. Therefore, we sometimes get nervous and anxious. Learning how to be a better strategic networker can help mitigate those fears.

Additionally, training in strategic networking can serve us well on those occasions when serendipity creates an unexpected networking opportunity. Nothing is planned, so there are no expectations, and there isn't any time to get nervous. When it's all over, we can sit back and take a deep breath. Often that is when what happened hits us.

The word *serendipity* comes from the Persian fairy tale *The Three Princes of Serendip.* "They were always making discoveries, by accident and sagacity, of things which they were not in quest of."[1] It is now defined as, "the faculty or phenomenon of finding valuable or agreeable things not sought for."[2]

Strategic networking prepares us for the serendipitous moments. When we are confident of our ability to meet people and explore a mutually beneficial relationship, we are more likely to be open to chance encounters and convert them to mutually beneficial relationships.

Summary: When you are confident of your networking ability, you are most ready to be spontaneous.

STATISTICS

What experience are your clients having with the people in your company? We don't do business with a company, we do business with people, usually people that we like. If that relationship sours, the firm earns less money and people lose their jobs. People are the deciding factor. Either they make a contribution to the business or they are a drain. It all goes back to people. Look at these numbers:

- 15 percent of customers switch products to get a lower price.
- 15 percent switch because they find a better product.

- 70 percent leave because of the human interaction of doing business with that vendor.[3]

These numbers are quite telling. The same people skills that make a good networker are also critical in retaining clients or customers! Sandler Sales Institute conducted a study on the impact of a personal introduction on the sales cycle. The study determined that

- Only 1 to 5 percent of cold calls lead to a successful sale.
- About 15 percent of referrals are successful when a name is given out. (E.g., I haven't worked with Susan before, but I know that her business helps start-ups create Web sites.)
- The success rate leaps to 50 percent when a phone call or e-mail is sent on your behalf.
- It catapults to the high 70s and over 80 percent when the person who can make the introduction attends the meeting or participates in the phone call.

These results are shown in Figure 2-2.

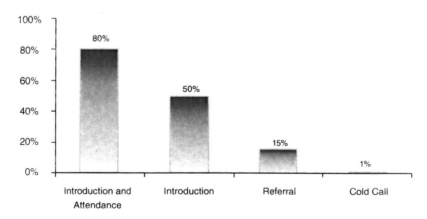

Figure 2-2   Value of Networking versus Cold Calls

I called Jack to get his advice on a business idea. We had worked together a few times, and I can always trust him to tell it to me straight. "I'm not the person who can help you, Matt is," he said. "Let's get him on the line." The next thing I knew, I was part of a three-way conversation. I had never even met Matt. Jack explained why Matt would benefit from the business idea. At first Matt wasn't convinced and was dismissive. Jack addressed his concerns, and at the end I had a new relationship with Matt—and I had talked the least!

Summary: The more people savvy you are, the better your chances of success. The more you let others help you, the greater your success.

3

Getting Started

Conditions are never just right. People who delay action until all factors are favorable are the kind who do nothing.

~ WILLIAM FEATHER

Most people begin to network when they need something—a job, a business lead, an employee, or a contribution to an organization. Effective networkers start *before they need something.* If you are networking now, good job! Keep it up. If you are not networking, start today. In order to receive, you must give. The more you have given to others, the easier and faster it will be to receive something from someone in your network when you have a genuine need.

Networking is progressive, and you can start it at any time. Too often, we undervalue ourselves, assuming that we cannot help someone else. Not so! Often, seeing how the little things we do for someone else are valued teaches us the real value of our knowledge. The more we give, the more we realize how easy it is to do so. It's also important to learn how to ask for help. Later in the book, I'll show you specific ways to request assistance.

Many networking resources tell you to make a list of your friends, work colleagues, family, and other contacts and start calling people. But I'm going to ask you to do something else first—talk to complete strangers.

Strangers? The idea may seem counterintuitive. However, can you remember a time when you were on a plane, and by the end of the flight, you knew the life story of the person sitting next to you? You were safe to talk to. The person didn't know you and therefore felt that he could talk to you about anything.

Put this book down and go for a walk or an errand. Smile and make eye contact with at least two people you don't know. People with dogs are typically very friendly. If you see someone with a dog, smile, walk up to her, and ask the animal's name. Start the conversation by asking if you can pet the dog. Next ask what the dog's breed is and how long the person has had the dog. After a few minutes, say thank you and then walk away.

Next, go to the grocery store and shop for some food. While you are selecting a brand, ask someone in the aisle if he is familiar with the product or if there is another brand that he prefers. Again thank the person and walk away.

The purpose of these two exercises is to get you to talk to someone you've never spoken to before and ask a few questions. You are not asking this person to become a client, to fund your business, or to get you a job. That's a sales call, an investment presentation, or a job interview. You are asking about a dog and about some groceries. You are also asking about the person or showing that you value her opinion.

Now, go do it. This will take only 10 to 15 minutes for each exercise.

How did it go? Ask yourself a few questions and note your answers:

- What did you like about the exercises?
- After the first few questions, what happened to the conversation?
- Did you find out something more about these people?
- What area of town do they live in?
- What do they do for a living?
- How did you feel when the exercise was over and you picked up this book again?
- Did you wish you could talk to strangers all day?
- What didn't you like?
- How did it feel walking up to a total stranger?
- What would you do differently?

You have just accomplished one of the key elements in successful networking: communicating with a stranger and making a connection. That is where networking begins, and the more you do it, the more confidence you'll gain. As with any kind of exercise, you need to develop those networking "muscles." The muscle memory will help you do it more easily and better the next time.

As you gain confidence in your networking ability, repeat the exercise, but this time with acquaintances—for example, people that you rarely see, perhaps a former colleague or someone you would just like to get to know better in business.

Asking for help from people we are close to can be quite intimidating. We assume that they know what we do and what we need. However, we can also miss an easy solution by not letting friends and family know what we are doing and how they can help us be successful.

Summary: Taking calculated risks has rewards. Test your networking skills on strangers. It is easier, since it's likely that you will be less nervous, and the risks are indeed much lower.

NETWORKING ONLINE

Many of these exercises are even easier online:

- What are some of your hobbies?
- Do you have pets?
- Are you interested in entrepreneurship or in learning a new language?

Go online and find communities or groups that share your interests. A great Web site for this that I use frequently is Meetup.com. If you have a dachshund, for example, you can meet other people who do, too. The majority of Meetup.com groups are designed to facilitate group activities in real life. Imagine how much easier meeting someone new would be if you already knew that you had a shared interest!

Starting online is great for several reasons:

- You can get to know people in advance so that you have conversation starters.
- You can explore a variety of options with no expense other than your time (but watch out—that can add up fast).
- You can read feedback and reviews of the groups and/or its past events.
- Based on the other groups that members of your groups have joined, you can identify other things that you might also enjoy.

Yahoo! groups are another good option for finding groups of people who share your interests. Free services like Ning.com allow you to set up online forums for real-time discussion of topics and are quickly replacing the e-mail-based discussion groups or "listservs" that were common in the 1980s and 1990s.

For safety's sake, always try to attend a first group activity at a public venue. If you feel that something is amiss, leave immediately. You can also invite a friend to go along.

ONLINE NETWORKING TOOLS

In this section I briefly describe a few of the most popular services in the growing category of social networking tools (a phrase that seems redundant to me, but okay). I'll be examining most of these later in the book, but this will provide an introduction if you are not familiar with them.

LinkedIn

LinkedIn is the most business-oriented of the social networking sites. It can be a phenomenal tool if you use it well. Its greatest benefit is in making members more aware of the connections within their network. It might take several conversations with a new acquaintance to learn that he is very good friends with an executive at a firm where you are applying or trying to secure a sales contract. LinkedIn will reveal it with a few clicks of the mouse.

Given its business focus, LinkedIn is where I focus on professional rather than personal networking. The site is a repository for my work experience, a place where people can post testimonials. I can upload slides or share information about my work. In addition, I can host or join groups that are related to my professional interests. I can add value and build credibility by answering questions on business topics posted by other members. In short, it's where you'll find me in a business suit!

Members can choose to make their profiles, activities on the site, and personal LinkedIn networks (connections) private. There's some debate about whether or not to hide one's network. As noted earlier, the networking power of the service is exponentially greater when you and your fellow members can see "who knows whom."

For this reason, most people make it possible for connections to see their entire LinkedIn network. (*Note:* LinkedIn blocks access to nonmembers and members who are not in your network, regardless of your privacy settings.)

An important issue in the world of online networking is the blurring of the line between one's professional and one's personal life. Because people are online at home and at work, it can be easy to forget one's networking manners! At a birthday party I attended, I was bringing out the cake to the party. The person holding the door for me happened to be a LinkedIn connection. As I was going through, the first thing he said was, "Diane, I meant to ask you. I saw on LinkedIn that you know Andrea, and I was wondering if you can introduce me, as I'd like to work there."

Jeez—at least let me put the cake down! That's not the best time to ask for a professional favor. Some people might say that online networking is the source of the rude behavior. I would reply that people were being rude or pushy long before the World Wide Web. However, our growing ability to share in others' lives through social networking makes it easier to get a bit too personal or be seen as inappropriate, so exercise good sense.

Let's back up. Imagine that David and I worked together about three years ago; we had fun, and he was a good colleague. I see on LinkedIn that David knows Andrea, and I'd like to network with her. What's the best way to make that happen?

Here's my suggestion: call David! Use it as an excuse to connect with him. Say hello and find out what's new in his life. Let him know why you want to network with Andrea—be 100 percent honest. Ask if he would be willing to send an e-mail or put in a call on your behalf, or if it is okay to mention his name in the conversation.

This is a case of effective *hybrid* networking. It may start online, then go to the phone, and then perhaps in person. The important thing is to identify a channel with which you are both most comfortable and a time when it's appropriate to discuss networking opportunities.

I'll get into more detail regarding using LinkedIn later in the book.

Facebook

Facebook's name and early history as a students-only site have resulted in many people regarding the service as being suited only for young people. It might surprise you to learn that the fastest-growing segment of Facebook users is people over 45! I know one woman of nearly 90 who uses it to stay connected with her many grandchildren.

Lots of people express their concerns about privacy on Facebook. Think of it this way ... only share online what you'd share in a restaurant. Anything can be overheard or misinterpreted in both places. If you don't want people to know, then don't post it.

Having said that, Facebook can be a terrific way to reconnect with lost friends. And that's the key word—friend! If you asked 20 people to define a friend, you would probably hear 20 different examples.

Here are a few of my filters on whether or not someone is a friend:

1. We have or have had some connection—personal or professional.
2. You can put a face to a name.
3. You know generally where I am located (e.g., New York versus Tokyo).
4. You know if I have a spouse/partner or children.
5. You are there for me on bad days as well as good.
6. You know what I do for a living.
7. In a pinch, you would loan me money! You might even help me move!

Okay, that last one is a bit of a stretch. But seriously, your friendship has value. While it would be ideal to be connected to the entire world, ask yourself a few questions before you invite or respond to a "friend" request.

Twitter

Another social networking site that has been making headlines recently is Twitter. Twitter bills itself as a "microblogging" site, with all messages restricted to 140 characters. In that sense, it is more similar to text messaging than to a rich media site like Facebook. Twitter and its appeal can seem a bit mystifying to nonusers and even many *new* users of the service. Messages are public—anyone can see them on what is called "the public timeline"—but the sheer quantity of messages can be daunting. In the section "Twitter," in Chapter 12, I'll explain how to use Twitter more effectively.

> *Summary: Online social networking platforms like LinkedIn, Facebook, and Twitter can turbocharge your networking efforts.*

CREATE A PLAN

> *Poor planning on your part does not create an emergency on my part.*
>
> ~ UNKNOWN

Pick a goal you want to achieve for which networking would be helpful. Maybe it's getting a new client or a new job. If you are involved with a nonprofit, perhaps you want to secure a grant or find more volunteers. Or maybe you have recently moved, and you want to take up a new sport—perhaps tennis or golf.

Throughout *The Networking Survival Guide*, we'll discuss your goal and ways to achieve it. Perhaps on the path you will discover a nice detour. This happens all the time. We have a specific purpose in mind; however, as the journey continues, something wonderful surprises us, and we now have a new objective.

While it's important to have goals, don't make them so rigid that you can't switch gears if a better opportunity comes along or if it is just necessary to make a change. Lisa went to a conference. Her goal was to get sales leads, but it turned out that the attendees were not at her level. At first she was disappointed; however, after hearing the first speaker, she felt inspired. She shifted her goal from sales to personal development rather than getting down on herself because she was spending time at a conference that wouldn't give her any new business.

No matter what you selected, your goals should be *smart*!

- S — specific
- M — measurable
- A — achievable
- R — realistic
- T — timed

What do I mean by "networking goals"? Here are some examples:

- ***Business development.*** Meet two people who can introduce me to decision makers who would want to purchase my product or service.
- ***Raising capital.*** Send an e-mail to my network sharing the news that we are seeking a $1 million expansion round of capital and asking people to help identify the right investors.
- ***Professional development.*** Contact three people who have a Master in Business Administration (MBA) and ask their advice about whether I should get one as well.
- ***Job search.*** Set up one-on-one meetings with two previous supervisors who know my skills.
- ***Recruiting.*** Hold an internal networking session at the office to let employees know of new jobs or a referral bonus plan for new hires.
- ***Nonprofit.*** Identify five donors who would like to donate to the Brain Tumor Society.

- *Social.* Call three health clubs in the city to which I
  have moved and get information about their members to
  determine which one is right for me.

You have identified why you want to network and what results
you are seeking. Now is the time to come down from the 10,000-
foot level and get practical. In order for us to start on our networking
journey, first we need to find the spot on the map that says, "You are
here!"

*Summary: When you plan, you save yourself time, energy,
and money, and ultimately you network smarter with less
effort.*

A FEW GOOD PEOPLE

Often I'm asked, "How many people do I need to know?" After all,
networking could quickly become a full-time job and then some. One
person can make quite a few introductions. Each person typically
knows about 200 to 250 people. If you add just one person to your
network each week, that would be 50 people in a year. If each of them
knows 200 other people, you automatically are two steps away from
10,000 people. Few people can manage that kind of interaction and
maintain high-quality networking.

Determine the type of people you want to add to your network.
Then find the locations where those people hang out. Everyone can
be useful in your life. Some are the decision makers, and others influence
them. What's most important is that they share your values and
that their actions reflect the quality of your life.

Your online network can be far larger than your "physical"
network—that is, people whom you can or do meet with face-to-face.
It's not unusual to see social networking users with tens or hundreds
of thousands of followers (Twitter) or friends (Facebook). Is this
network as strong as the traditional offline network? Of course not.

However, the scale of the online network can make it just as effective if the person is highly regarded (i.e., provides valuable content or services). These people may not have ever met face-to-face. But the content they produce—blog posts, links to useful articles, and so on—has made a great first impression and set the stage for a deeper relationship.

This is not to say that you can collect business cards or buy mailing lists and call the result your network. In the situation described in the previous paragraph, the individuals in question have already created value and earned credibility with their networks, even if the only contact is electronic. Think about the value you can provide and start building your own network in the same way.

Summary: You want high-quality contacts, not just quantity. Online networks can help you increase the number of contacts without sacrificing quality.

INVENTORY YOUR NETWORKS

I often teach business school students who are brilliant and ambitious. I ask them to pull out a piece of paper and start writing down the names of the people who encouraged them to get a MBA. I tell them to include everyone from the postman who delivered the acceptance letter to the person who first suggested that it would be a good career move.

I then ask them to review the list and recall when was the last time they were in contact with each of the people on it. Their eyes start getting big, and there's a grimace or two.

You need to start with the people you know.

When I ask clients to inventory their networks, many say that they have only one network. Typically, that network is business-related. By the end of a few sessions, however, they realize that they have many more networks than they thought they had.

When you have identified and organized your networks, it's easier to find the right person for the right problem. You can also start introducing people to each other. You are then viewed as a go-to person, and you become a networking "node."

Most of us have a toothbrush holder in the bathroom and a place where we put our forks, typically in the kitchen. It would be quite miserable if they got mixed up. This is what can happen when we mix our networks: we get a fork in our gums. Ouch!

When a company creates an organization chart, it simply identifies the roles that the firm needs in order to run effectively, and this allows it to put the right people in the right jobs.

You are going to inventory your networks. This is a useful exercise that is fundamental to your networking plan. You will quickly realize that you know more people than you thought you did. As you do this exercise, note people's interests. For example, as you map your network, you'll recall that your good friend from college is an avid sailor. You'll realize that one of your work colleagues and also one of your neighbors have sailboats. This will give you a perfect excuse to introduce people to each other. You can send an e-mail to each person introducing the others, saying what they have in common, and telling them how each person can meet the other.

Why make the effort? This is an excellent way to increase your visibility in your community. You will become known as a go-to person. When people have a problem that they need solved, they will come to you. This extends your value.

This is an investment in your community and your business success.

Figure 3-1 is an example of what a network looks like. In order to do the inventory exercise, you need

- A piece of paper—consider getting something a bit larger, like a poster size
- A pen or pencil
- Post-it notes—different sizes or colors are helpful (or an eraser)

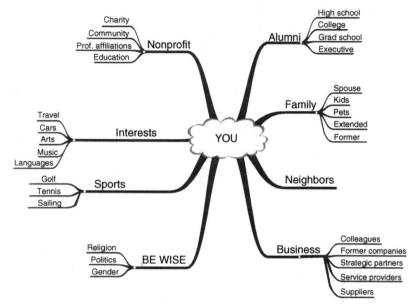

Figure 3-1   Map Your Network

Let's begin:

1. ***In the middle of the paper, write your name in the cloud.*** (See the example in Figure 3-1.) Now you know the truth: you are the center of the universe!

2. ***Next, determine what networks you have.*** For example:

   a. *Alumni.* List all the schools you have affiliations with and where you've stayed in touch with people. What are they up to now? Think of people who can be a resource for you and vice versa.

   b. *Neighbors.* This is often an overlooked category. Often we know little about the people who live near us, yet obviously we have a lot in common or we wouldn't have selected the neighborhood to begin with.

   c. *Family.* Kids and pets are a hidden gem in this category. Through them we can meet all kinds of interesting people. One's extended family is also a terrific resource. There can be a more friendly relationship in many cases.

d. *Business.* This is the core network that we will review. Don't forget about your previous companies. Corporate alumni groups are strong and loyal. This is an excellent resource for you to connect with.

e. *Nonprofit.* There are many wonderful people you will meet who participate in a variety of nonprofits. These organizations attract a cross section of people who share a common interest but come from a wide variety of industries.

f. *Interests.* Where to stop, there are so many! This is often where business relationships begin. People start talking and realize that they share a common interest. Even if you don't participate, read about trends and what's going on.

g. *Sports.* Almost everyone has a sport that she either follows or participates in. For me, the day after the Super Bowl is a somber one—I just love football. The strategy, passion, and energy are enjoyable to me. I'm not particularly athletic, so I try to learn tennis every so often.

h. *Be wise!* You'll notice that there is one branch on the chart that reads, "be wise." These are the people in three specific networks: politics, religion, and gender. It is important to manage these relationships carefully. While you may guess that someone else who practices your faith has the same political opinions as you do, it is prudent to be wise.

Pick one of the networks, let's say business. (If you want, use Post-it notes the first time you work on this exercise until you get the hang of it.)

3. *As you identify your network, organize it.* This will be a living document—in other words, as your life changes, so will your networking inventory. Just like writing a business plan, the first time you do it will be the most work.

4. *Start with one network*—for example, former colleagues—*and do a complete inventory.*

   a. Write the name of each person.

   b. As you are doing this, think of each person's hobbies, profession, and so on.

   c. What do you know about each person?

   d. What does each person know about you?

   e. Will each person return your call? If so, how quickly? If not, why not?

   f. Whom are you comfortable calling?

   g. Whom would you not call? Why?

5. *Take a break. Stop and take a look at the bigger picture of who is in your network.*

6. *Make a list of people to introduce to each other.*

   a. Why would they like to meet?

   b. What are their common links?

While it is valuable to inventory these groups, be careful how much you "cross-network," if you will. Unless you know that two people share a cause, doing so is a quick way to lose friends or business. You may have strong feelings about a certain political issue, and if you aren't careful, you can alienate both friends and business associates.

One time I was at a "woman" event at the Kennedy Library. The panel included four incredible women who were considered trailblazers in their respective fields. At the time, the governor of Massachusetts was a woman who had recently had twins while she was in office. Opinions ran the gamut on whether she was a trailblazer or whether she confirmed the suspicion some people had that women shouldn't hold public office.

I stood up to ask the women panelists what they thought of her and how she was being treated. The silence in the room was truly deafening; then there were a few hushed boos and hisses. I sat down and asked the person sitting next to me what was going on. "Diane, you asked a question about a Republican. We are at the Kennedy Library."

Summary: Inventory and organize your network. Take good care of it.

EVALUATE YOUR NETWORK

Now that you know who is in your network, it's time to evaluate each contact, his relationship to what you need, and, of course, how you can give back. Since each relationship is unique, your assessment will be unique as well.

For each person, ask yourself how accessible she is and whether your call will be returned promptly (within 48 hours). Networking is more than whom you know. It's who knows you! This delicate difference becomes much more evident when you don't get a return call.

Networking gives you ways to stay in touch and helps you discover who those people in your life are. This is not a popularity contest like high school. This is not *just* about people we like; it's more than that. It's about people we can get help from when we need it and vice versa.

There are some basic criteria to use for everyone:

- *How does he make me feel?*
  - Am I energized or drained after being with her?
  - Do I feel valued?
  - Does he treat me with respect?

- ○ Am I heard?
- ○ Do I laugh when I'm with her?
- ○ Do I have fun?
- ○ Am I given worthwhile feedback, or do I feel criticized?
- ○ What is his temper like? I find it exhausting when I'm on edge wondering if or when someone will be angry or moody.
- **Is her knowledge relevant to my present needs?**
  - ○ Does this person have expertise that I need right now?
  - ○ Will he be willing and able to make time for me?
  - ○ Does she have access to others who can be of assistance?
- **What can I give back?**
  - ○ Is there someone I can introduce him to?
  - ○ Is there an organization or event that I can tell her about?
  - ○ What compensation would this person like? For some, it is cash; in other cases, it's another currency—introductions, advice, referrals, time, or something else. Get his input.

Either people make you feel good or they don't. It's just that simple. This doesn't mean that you will always be told that it's going to be a beautiful sunny day and everything is rosy. In fact, we often feel the most cared for when people are willing to give us heartfelt, genuine feedback. We are treated with respect, and both parties are valued.

Do you have the right relationships in place for the achievement you are seeking? Here are some questions that are worth reviewing:

- Who has the power to help you (power as in access)?
- What do you need from these people? Have you written it down?
- What is the best way to approach them? Who can make an introduction on your behalf?

- What is your value? What problem do you solve?
- What is their value? What do they offer you?

Company or Organization

Evaluate the companies or organizations you have affiliations with. The goal is to get a bird's-eye view of the relationship. This includes metrics such as

- Have you earned new clients through your association with this organization?
- Who was instrumental in making that happen?
- If the company or organization is a key client, what would happen if your contact left? Do you have other relationships in place?
- Has someone in the organization introduced you to someone you hired?
- Did someone in the organization introduce you to a new supplier?

For organizations where you volunteer, ask the same questions. In addition, what is your role with the group? Write it out. What is the value you offer and get?

- What have you accomplished for the organization?
- How much time do you contribute?
- When you look on your calendar and see that you have a meeting with the group, does that make you feel energized or drained?
- How long have you been involved with the group?
- Is there a natural successor to you? If not, why not? Consider finding one and mentoring her—this will get you visibility.

- How did you get involved in the beginning?
- Has the relationship served its purpose, or is there still more you can accomplish?

Figure 3-2 shows the company; we will do the people next. Create a profile for each company.

People

As you already know, you do business with people, not with companies or organizations. Now we want to drill down and evaluate the people in each company or organization.

On each Post-it note, write three things:

- CB—this means that the person will call you back within a week.

Corporate Profile

Company	$ spent with them
Address	Services provided
City, State, Zip	
Main phone	
Web	
Industry	
Contact name	CEO name
Title	Last time we spoke
Last time met F2F	Last time we met F2F
Introduced by?	
Met where?	
Referred biz to us?	
Outcome?	
Sent thank-you?	
Referred employee?	

Figure 3-2   Corporate Profile

- What you can offer the person (underline it).
- What you want from the person (put it in quotes).

To start, create a business profile for the top and bottom 5 percent of your clients based on revenue or profitability. Get to know them a bit better. Review these questions and see what you know off the top of your head:

- Who are their service providers?
- When was the last time you met with them and didn't ask for anything?
- What significant milestones have they met or are likely to meet soon?
- Did you send a congratulations gift or take them to dinner?
- Have they made a hire recently whom you haven't met?

Make a list of the companies that are in the bottom 5 percent *and* have people whom you genuinely like doing business with. These people will help you practice new networking skills. To start out, ask yourself,

- Why do you like them?
- What can you do to make them more successful?
- Whom can you introduce them to?

Make this an excellent learning opportunity for networking. Much of what you will learn is how much you can give to others and how much they would be delighted to help you. You just have to ask!

Do the same with your top 5 percent. Don't make calls to them right away, though.

Summary: Build relationships BEFORE you need them!

NETWORKING WITH PRESENT CLIENTS

Now that you've successfully inventoried and prioritized your present clients, you know what works for your business and what doesn't. After a few networking sessions, you also have a good idea of what patterns you see in your clients, what their needs are, and how you can help. In addition, you are learning ways in which they can help you. The more information you have, the easier it is for you to ask for their support. In order to maximize your time and effort, here is a strategy you can use as a template.

1. ***Prepare.*** Put together a three- or four-bullet-point outline about the person you are contacting and what you want from him. For example,

   a. Calling Jack Jones.

   b. Want introduction to Ms. Smith @ Smith & Associates.

   c. Would like to provide legal services.

   d. We have expertise in mergers and acquisitions and can help her grow the company.

   Do some online research about Smith & Associates. Is Ms. Smith on any boards? What are some of her charities? A quick search online will make your preparation better. Please remember that there could be more than one Ms. Smith. And also realize that not everything you read online is true.

   There are several other Diane Darlings out there. One is an acne specialist, another is a doll collector, and another is a motorcycle collector, to name just a few. Over a meeting, someone asked me a question about motorcycles, which was confusing for me and embarrassing for him.

2. ***E-mail and call to ask for a meeting.*** Yes, I suggest that you do both. E-mail is overwhelming and can get lost. Do a hybrid outreach by also calling and letting the person

hear your voice. It feels more personal. Refer to the
e-mail so that she doesn't have to take any notes, she just
needs to look up your e-mail and get an answer back to
you.

3. ***Let the person know why you are contacting him***—for
   example, that you are growing your business and would
   like his advice.

4. ***Set the meeting according to what's best for the other
   person***—location, time, and so on.

5. ***Pick up the tab for any expenses.***

6. ***At the meeting, do the following:***

   a. *Be very specific.* If you want an introduction to the vice
      president of marketing at a certain company, know that
      person's name and why you want to meet her.

   b. *Create an atmosphere in which the person can say no.*
      Make it comfortable for him to say that the timing isn't
      right or the relationship isn't such that he can do what
      you ask.

   c. *WII-FM—what's in it for this person?* Why should he
      help you? Is there a compelling reason?

7. ***After the meeting, do the following:***

   a. *Send a thank-you note within 24 to 48 hours.* Use e-mail
      or paper, whichever is more appropriate.

   b. *Keep the person updated on your progress.*

   c. *Ask what you can do for her.*

8. ***Repeat steps 1 to 7 with each client.***

NET VERSUS GROSS

I'm not sure how I would define *grossworking* even if I had to! Fortunately, as with our income, the net is what we really care about.

It is what we get to keep. We refer to our safety net as a source of protection, a resource for us.

From lemonade stand proprietors to *Fortune* 100 CEOs, the difference between net and gross on a balance sheet is where the truth is told. Few people realize that the same principle applies to a network. When you take a look at all the people in your Rolodex (the gross) or contact database and subtract the people with whom you have the fewest reciprocal relationships, you arrive at the net. In other words, you want to focus on those people with whom you have the most in common. These are the people you can help the most, and vice versa. This is your true "net" network.

Sales professionals call this the 80/20 rule: you get 80 percent of your business from 20 percent of your clients.

A question that often comes up is how to purge names. I'm actually a believer in reorganizing rather than eliminating. I worked in the travel industry for a number of years, and I met a wide variety of fun and wonderful people. Now, however, we are no longer colleagues. As I reinventory my network, these people move to a new group— vendors, friends, acquaintances, or some other category.

As you complete the inventory exercise, you have a visual reminder that networks are fluid and ever-changing. Whenever I look at my database, I am always thinking, who would like to meet whom? This is also an opportunity to reconnect with someone without stalking her. (See the section "The Difference between Persistence and Stalking," in Chapter 11.)

Summary: Who are the core members of your network, and what do you offer them? What do they offer you?

HOW TO PRIORITIZE WITH WHOM YOU NETWORK AND WHY

Now that we have identified and evaluated the network, let's prioritize it and focus on the "net." We want to learn more about these people—

what we have to offer each other, and why. People drive companies and organizations. They move from one to another, and ultimately all our relationships are with the person, not the company.

Now we need to do another exercise that is similar to the others, but that is focused on the individuals, not the firm. (See Figure 3-3.)

Personal Profile

BUSINESS		Allergies/injuries	
Name	_____	Family situation	_____
Title	_____	Custom/culture	_____
Name of company	_____		
Business address	_____	PERSONAL	
City, State, Zip	_____	Phone	_____
Phone	_____	E-mail	_____
E-mail	_____	Spouse/S.O.	_____
Facebook	_____	Children	_____
LinkedIn	_____	Spouse's job	_____
Twitter	_____	Spouse's college	_____
Web	_____	Grad school	_____
What his/her job is	_____	Children's school	_____
Latest promotion	_____	Children's sports	_____
Sent congratulations	_____	Children's awards	_____
College	_____	Community involvement	_____
Grad school	_____	Spouse referred biz	_____
Associations	_____	Family pet	_____
Charities	_____	Name	_____
Board	_____	Breed	_____
Hobbies	_____		
Sports	_____		
Awards	_____		
Referred any biz	_____		
Things to know	_____		

Phone: 888-907-0900   ©2010 Effective Networking, Inc.
E-mail: Info@EffectiveNetworking.com

Figure 3-3   Personal Profile

- Whom do you like?
- Who gives you business?
- Whom do you give business to, and why?
- Who makes introductions on your behalf?
- Who returns your calls?
- Who is fun?
- Who makes you feel good?
- Who makes you feel stupid?
- Who is on the executive team?
- Where did each person go to college or graduate school?
- What community organizations is each person involved with? What professional associations? What nonprofit boards?
- Where do each person's children go to school?

Now it's time to put this into action. Go to the list of clients that you like. That's right, people that you just like, whether or not they are key customers from a revenue perspective. The two of you have worked together for a while and built a rapport, as well as a trust. Ask each of these people to meet you for breakfast or lunch (find out what is best for each particular person). I would encourage you to stay away from your top 5 percent. Select from the bottom 5 to 30 percent of your list. The goal is to practice networking, and you don't want to be practicing on your top clients. The more you do this, the better and more comfortable you will be. Don't risk nerves in your first few meetings.

Tell your client about this project and why you are doing it. What would you like from this person? Why did his name pop into your mind—do you want business leads or a job? Enlist his support. Explain that you want to take your career, business, or organization to the next level, and that you realize the importance of widening your professional community. Ask his advice. Following each meeting, determine your next steps by asking yourself the following:

- Is this someone you should meet with on a regular basis— once a week, month, quarter, or year?
- What can you do to help this person?
- What did you learn from the meeting?
- Would you do anything differently? If so, what and why?

People grow and change throughout their life. It is worthwhile reviewing your networks periodically to see whether you have people in the right place for mutual success. For example, there may be someone you worked with many years ago. You were in different departments, but you commuted together. Now you learn that your firm is seeking a new head of product development. That individual was in your colleague network, then shifted to your acquaintance network, and now is a potential work colleague again.

It is easy to overlook the people in your present network. You can quickly exhaust yourself meeting new people when your present clients may have the answers to your questions and just need to be asked. In addition, you may determine that a relationship needs to shift into a different network. Or you may decide that your time is better invested in other things and it's time for someone else to take over this relationship.

Summary: By continually prioritizing your network, you will discover what is the best use of your time—both for you and for your business—and who are the people who can help you succeed.

WHAT'S THE STATUS OF YOUR "NETBANK"?

If you want to connect with someone, but are hesitant to do so, maybe you should take a look at your "netbank" with that person. We have a netbank with everyone we know. Just as with a regular account at a bank, either there is a balance in the netbank or it's empty. The quickest way to find out if you have a balance in your netbank with someone is to try to make a withdrawal.

- When you need to call this person, do you feel free to do so?
- Will it be awkward for you to call? If so, why?
- Has it been a long time since you last spoke to this individual?
- When this person last called you, did you take the call— whether or not you could help him?

We have netbanks with people we have helped in the past. We may have made an introduction on their behalf, given them a job reference, made a contribution to their favorite charity, or introduced them to a tennis partner in their neighborhood, for example.

If you hesitate to pick up the phone, the balance in your netbank with that person is either nonexistent or too low. Here's how to remedy the situation:

- Make a commitment *now* to finding a way to make a deposit in your netbank with that person. Do this ASAP!
- Ask for nothing at this time. *Wait.*
- Simply find something that you can do for the person.
- Identify people that you have a netbank with. Can they help you? Will they help you? Why or why not?
- Take a look at your networking inventory. What is the status of your netbanks for others?

Consider the following three examples:

1. There is a prospect that you want to meet. Recently you learned that your former boss went to graduate school with this prospect. However, the last two times your former boss asked you to meet for coffee, you said you didn't have time.

2. You like to have a fresh cup of coffee from the specialty shop at the corner first thing each morning. Every so often, the person sitting in the office next to you comments that she should go out and get a cup of coffee, but she is just too busy. Yesterday you picked up two cups and gave one to your colleague.

3. You are considering a job change. Last time, you were placed by an executive search firm. However, you got so busy with the position that you never sent a thank-you note or updated the recruiter on your success. Now you are miserable, and you want to call the recruiter to get some help.

Which of these people have deposits in their netbank? You got it right, the second person. It may seem like a little thing. (See the section, "What Falling on Your Face Can Teach You about Networking," in Chapter 4.) However, when you call your colleague from the airport and say, "Would you please get the confidential memo I left on the printer and put it in my desk drawer?" What do you think will happen?

Summary: Start making deposits now. They don't have to be huge or elaborate. A friendly smile or a five-minute phone call can go a long way.

UNCLUTTER YOUR NETWORK

For nearly 15 years, I worked in the travel industry. I met some amazing people. Then I changed industries. I still see those people on occasion, but now we connect as friends.

On an ongoing basis, check your inventory and be sure that people are in the right network. There may be times when it makes sense to move someone from a business network category to a personal one, or from a personal to an acquaintance network. Sometimes business or personal relationships outlive the need for them.

This doesn't mean that you dislike this person; it just means that he belongs in a different place in your life.

How many relationships can you manage and handle them well? While we want to keep our network fresh and inspired, we can quickly have too much going on. The next thing we find is that we have too many commitments to too many people and nothing is well managed.

People We Hear From Only when They Need Something

We all know the drill. The phone rings, and there is a very friendly voice on the other end wanting to know what we've been up to. We engage in the conversation waiting for the request to come, and it almost always does. There are indeed people whom we hear from only when they want something from us. Determine what your tolerance level for these people is and how much brain space you allow them to occupy rent-free.

Unhealthy People (or Forget about It!)

Throughout our lives, we will meet people whom we don't connect with or who are just not healthy and/or helpful. In some cases they can actually distract us. In some cases we continue to stay associated with them for a variety of reasons. Perhaps it's a challenge, or perhaps we think we need to for some reason.

These individuals are a bit more complex. They latch themselves onto us, and we permit them to do so. Like the folks we hear from only when they want something, these individuals add little or no value to our lives. In fact, sometimes they are downright destructive. They create conflict and gossip and are a distraction to you and those around you.

This is not a network to ignore. There's the saying, "Keep your friends close and your enemies closer." It's important to know who your detractors are. On occasion, it may be necessary to talk to them. By confronting people, we can often avoid a confrontation. The word *confront* has a negative connotation. The antonym is the word *avoid*.

When we don't express our concerns about how someone is treating us, she may not know that what she is doing is hurting us. When we avoid the situation, it often gets bigger and bigger in our minds. That can lead to internal anger, which, if unexpressed, can turn into depression.

What we need to do is learn how to express ourselves in a positive and productive way. What sometimes goes wrong is that we let out our pent-up frustration, and it's like taking a finger out of the hole in a dike. The power and thrust of the works are so strong that they shock the other person, and the relationship is damaged further instead of being repaired.

Find an interactive class in negotiation. Be sure you have a chance to participate actively. It's not enough to sit back and watch. This is one of the best things you'll ever do for yourself.

If you find yourself blowing up at people, then a class in anger management may be an option. The truth is that everyone gets angry, and everyone should. It's how the anger is expressed that determines what happens next.

In some cases it's necessary for you to be the bigger person and just walk away. As when two people are playing catch, simply put down the ball and refuse to play. It isn't worth your time and energy.

> *Summary: Sometimes it's just best to think of yourself as Robert DeNiro and say, "Forget about it!"*

Grandpa's Shoes

When I was a little girl, I remember my friend's grandfather talking about his two pairs of shoes—a black pair and a brown pair. He could well afford to have more, but that was all he needed. I remember hearing him tell someone about how he took care of his shoes. Each night he would put powder in them to keep them fresh and put shoe trees in them to maintain their shape.

When I walk into stores these days, I'm often overwhelmed by all the things I can buy and how much I could have in my life if I wanted to. It's easy to trick ourselves into believing that we never have enough. We need more. When purchasing things isn't expensive, we tend to buy more. Almost everything comes in a disposable version. [Mind you, for some products (e.g., diapers), this is a monumental improvement.]

However, it can be easy to think that way about our networks. Instead of caring for and investing in a few good, strategic relationships in business, we kid ourselves into believing that we have a huge support network, when it really is just acquaintances.

Many people have a Rolodex or contact database that is full of names. The question is, now what? How many of them do you really know? How many of them do you really want to help? Which of them would help you if you called? If someone doesn't know much about you, what he can do for you, and what you can do for him, then the relationship is limited.

Summary: Surround yourself with high-quality people—they are your networking halo. You are the company you keep. Realize that as you succeed, there will be some people who are not happy with your success. Let them go and fly with eagles who want you to soar.

Dr. Ruth Has Some Networking Advice

Dr. Ruth Westheimer, Psychologist

She measures 4'7", has the stamina of the Energizer Bunny, and will turn 80 in June. Her voice has been described as a cross between Minnie Mouse and Henry Kissinger. Dr. Ruth Westheimer is quite an expert on, well . . . people skills.

I met Dr. Ruth on a recent trip to New York City. We grabbed a cab in mid-afternoon and headed to one of her favorite restaurants, Paynard's, on the Upper East Side. Her ability to connect with others was immediately obvious. She greeted Fabrice, the maitre d', in his native French, explaining that she was being interviewed and asking which table would be best. The next thing I knew, we were escorted into an empty dining room where they were clearing a table that had been preset for the evening. We settled in while Fabrice brought her a pillow to sit on. The coffee arrived and the conversation began.

Let me share with you some of Dr. Ruth's observations:

Unrealistic expectations. Super people skills are essential in order to avoid disappointment. Many of life's letdowns occur because we have unrealistic expectations of others. We want people to be something for us that they are just not going to be. The disappointment comes because we create an idea of who they are supposed to be, and our image gets deflated. It is not necessarily their fault; it is the idealistic notions that we create. Use your networking skills to get a realistic sense of the individuals you meet.

Handling disappointment. Dr. Ruth knows about disappointment. She was orphaned as a child when her family was killed in the Holocaust. She went on to live in a kibbutz in Israel (where she learned sharpshooting) before immigrating to the United States. She feels strongly that while she must not forget the horror, she has an equal obligation to do what she can with her talents because she survived. Her eyes sparkled when she said, "I need to make a difference. I need to do something positive because I lived. I am very fortunate and do not take anything for granted."

Self-confidence. Dr. Ruth talked about the importance of developing a sense of self so that you can withstand life's ups and downs. This helps when the people in your network come and go, especially in unpredictable ways. A strong sense of self keeps us from falling apart so that we can dust ourselves off and continue on with our lives.

Good role models. Dr. Ruth noted the advantage for the young of having good role models, particularly of how to treat others. Children observe their parents and teachers dealing with one another, as well as with service personnel such as administrative staff, restaurant workers, and cleaners. If respect for others, no matter what their station in life, is lacking, children miss an essential lesson that carries into adulthood. This impedes their people skills.

Mistakes. I asked Dr. Ruth what mistakes she thought people make. She said that we are too impatient; we need to slow down and take a breath. We expect everything instantly, and not only is this unrealistic, but in many ways it is counterproductive. She said she found it odd that two people would walk down the street together, each listening to an iPod. Why aren't they speaking to each other?

Be a mischievous listener. Dr. Ruth was once given an award for "mischievousness in listening." She was thrilled. There are many people who do lots of talking. However, few of us actually listen—we might hear, but that is not the same thing. You need to really pay attention to what the other person is saying, rather than thinking about what you want to say in reply.

Conversations. Dr. Ruth encourages people to surround themselves with interesting people with whom they can have engaging conversations. She feels incredibly blessed that she has often been around a dinner table listening to others and learning fascinating things about their lives.

The TV Show **Sex and the City.** Dr. Ruth found the show quite humorous. How odd to think that New York City revolves around the lives of four women. She hopes people remember that this is just a TV show, not reality.

Parting words of advice. Be responsible for your own destiny. If there is something you want, ask for it. If you are rejected, do not get discouraged to the point that you stop reaching out. Empowering others to help you—without giving your power away—is the fastest way to get anything done. "After all," she said with a twinkle in her eye, "people cannot read your mind, so don't be ashamed to let them know how they can help you."

Meetup.com

Scott Heiferman, creator of Meetup.com

If you own a Chihuahua and want to meet others who do, a good place to look is Meetup.com. The same is true if you have toddlers, are single and want to meet someone, or just like to go to movies.

Meetup.com was inspired by the events of September 11. Scott Heiferman felt that there was a need to build community, both online and offline, so he created a place where people could do that. It's likely that there is someone else in your city with the same interests as you. Scott was inspired to create a place where people could actually meet in person, but leverage the Web to find each other.

I host several Meetups in Boston:

- *Drinks above Tiffany's* is exactly that. We meet for drinks at Legal Seafood, above Tiffany's in the Copley Mall in Boston. The purpose of the gathering is to give people a chance to practice networking with others who are also learning or who just want to be more comfortable attending events and approaching strangers.

    I've created an exercise where you introduce someone you've just met. The purpose is to hear what others think you do. After all, we can only be at one place at a time. If we have a fleet of ambassadors out there who know what we do, they can be on the lookout for professional or personal opportunities for us.

- *Boston ex-Midwesterners* is a group of people who find themselves away from home and want to talk to someone else who has no idea what a "bubbler" is. (It's Bostonian for water cooler.) We get together wearing name badges that give our name and state. Being Midwesterners, we are an extremely friendly lot, and you don't have to have a reason to say hello.

- *Boston ex-Westerners* was launched after my recent trip back to Colorado, where I lived as a kid. The mountain air and wide-open spaces are so inviting. When I got back, I bumped into several folks who longed for a networking group of like-minded people.

    If you find yourself in the Boston area, please join us!

I often travel around the country and speak to Meetup groups about how to network and maximize online and offline connections.

What's fascinating is that the Web allows people to self-select and find interest groups outside of their typical friendships. It's likely that the people you'll meet at work may share some of your professional interests. But it's uncertain that my work friends would have joined me for a class in fencing or an afternoon at a museum.

I also have found groups that share a common situation— motherless daughters or people with ADD. At times I find that I have a free afternoon, and instead of trying to figure out what to do, I often go to Meetup.com and see what are some events in the area.

If there isn't a group in your area, consider starting one. Find a friend to help you do the organizing. I've found that restaurants are very welcoming, especially on a Monday night. They put out appetizers and offer a cash bar, and I bring in a group of customers.

Give it a shot!

4

Preparing for Networking

When you're prepared, you're more confident. When you have a strategy, you're more comfortable.

~ FRED COUPLES

Recently in a meeting I heard the saying, "Proper planning prevents poor performance." It's such a refreshing statement. When it's curtain time—when your presentation, job interview, donation request, or investment presentation begins—you'll quickly get that feeling of either butterflies or calm confidence.

A significant amount of preparation can be done online. Research the person or organization ahead of time. Who are the stakeholders? What networks do they belong to? Where did they work in the past? Checking people out ahead of time used to be a bit creepy; now it's expected. Do your homework!

Next, let's look at some tactical ways to prepare and best practices to get your confidence anchored.

Spectacular achievement is always preceded by spectacular preparation.

~ ROBERT H. SCHULLER

YOUR SUPPORT NETWORKS

A client was heading off to an important industry conference with a work colleague. When they met at the event, he was startled. She was not dressed appropriately. Her clothes didn't quite match, and her attire was too casual. The situation was all the more awkward because she was senior to him. How do you tell someone that her clothes don't look right—especially when she's your boss?

Recall the discussion earlier. We have only a few seconds to make a first impression. Depending on your age, you may or may not remember the streaking craze on college campuses in the 1960s and 1970s. I was a budding teenage girl, and I thought this was just magnificent. I also remember a magazine that provided a guide for streakers. As I recall, the suggestions were as follows: "Wear a hat, ski goggles, and of course good running shoes. Last but not least, stand in front of a full-length mirror. After all, we want to keep America beautiful."

It's always been important for us to take care of our looks and our image. Packaging is just as important for people as it is for products. What's important is to maximize what you have. I have seen what some would call very beautiful women look completely unappealing, with a slouched posture, sloppy clothes, and a scowl. Yes, Denzel Washington is a great actor, but what a smile! When Bill Gates appeared in Washington, D.C., his clothes were professional, and his style was quite different from what we had become accustomed to seeing. Even David Letterman, Jay Leno, Conan O'Brien, Stephen Colbert, and Jon Stewart wear a suit when they work. Their guests may wear anything and everything, but that's not okay for the host.

"First Impressions," read the headline of the *Boston Globe* prior to the opening of Gillette Stadium in Foxborough, Massachusetts, home of the New England Patriots. There was less concern about the football. "There are bigger fish to fry. The Patriots' brass will be watching—and crossing their fingers—to see . . . how bad the traffic tie-ups will be outside the stadium."[1] Of course, the team wanted to win its first game after its surprise victory over the St. Louis Rams at Super Bowl XXXVI. However, it was equally critical for the event management crew, the concessionaires, the team owners—in short, the home team's "business" side—that the people attending the game had a wonderful experience at the new facility, even when it came to getting there!

A client begrudgingly hired an image consultant. She was deathly afraid of losing her personality and individuality in her clothes and style. Instead, it was a trip to freedom. She now had classic clothes that were appropriate for the audiences she worked with. Her clothes were no longer a daily distraction, not to mention a source of angst. Instead, she gained confidence and felt that she was more a part of the business community that she served.

Your friends are not your fashion advisors; nor are they responsible for telling you to change anything else about your person. Take charge. Find people who are specialists, hire them, and keep yourself up-to-date.

Create a "kick-off" networking support group. What is great about this is that you will learn things that are practical from each of these people, everything is easy to do, and you can learn this material *fast*. I call this my MMB Team—these people "make me better," or collectively, they are a "director of first impressions." This group builds your confidence.

Start from the outside and move in. Begin with your clothes, manners, image, fitness, and health. The people on this team are the keeper of your first impression. That's their job—let them do it. Get out of the way!

I've heard people say that fashion and even manners are "little things." Their position is, "It's more important that people get to know me for who I am." In a perfect world, that would be absolutely true. But we don't live in one, so we can either spend time fighting our culture or accept reality and invest in being our best, on the outside as well as on the inside.

What Falling on Your Face Can Teach You about Networking

If you are still not convinced, see how "little" things can keep you from falling flat on your face:

- Stand up.
- Lean forward as far as you possibly can without falling over. You may need to try this a few times.
- What is keeping you from actually falling on your face?
- Yes, balance plays a role. What else?
- Your toes!
- Now ask yourself, how big are your toes compared to the rest of your body?

Pretty little, huh? My point is that little things do matter. This includes appropriate attire, a proper handshake, good manners, and saying thank you. During the late 1990s and up to the year 2000, it was assumed that these things were "old-fashioned." However, taking care of these "little" things means that you can let others focus on the big things.

Say thank you to your toes. In honor of them, here are people you should hire and skills you should work on to help you make a winning first impression. (See Figure 4-1.)

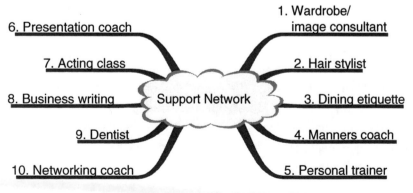

Figure 4-1 Support Network

1. ***Wardrobe/image consultant.*** This may be one person or perhaps more.

    a. *Wardrobe.* It's getting more and more difficult to know what to wear these days. What does business casual actually mean? Hire a specialist to go through your closet. Put together several outfits that are appropriate for various circumstances and various times of the year. This actually makes getting dressed for work much easier.

    b. *Image.* Glasses or contacts? Beard or no beard? Short hair or long? What color makeup? Find someone who can walk you through the choices and give you professional advice on your image beyond your clothes.

2. ***Hair stylist.*** Yale University did a study about the impact on our self-esteem if we have a "bad hair day." Gentlemen, it turns out you feel the same way. The three take-aways from the study were

    a. *Bad hair lowers self-esteem regarding performance.* "The perception of bad hair leads to a reduced sense of performance self-esteem. Just the thought of a bad hair day caused both men and women to feel they are not as smart as others. Surprisingly, the impact . . . was more pronounced among men."

    b. *Bad hair increases social insecurity.* "Women tend to feel more disgraced, embarrassed, ashamed or self-conscious. Men feel more nervous, less confident, and are inclined to be unsociable."

    c. *Bad hair intensifies self-criticism.* "Evidence shows that bad hair causes one to be more negative about oneself."[2]

    Find a stylist who listens. Find someone whose hair you like and ask where she gets it cut. Then forget about it—it's just one of your toes! How often do you think about them?

3. ***Dining etiquette.*** Remember in the movie *Pretty Woman* when Julia Roberts's character asks the hotel general manager to teach her how to eat properly? Fine restaurants and hotels are teaching classes these days. Refresh your etiquette and meet some nice people in the process. Sign up!

4. ***Manners coach.*** For those of you who were fans of *The West Wing*, you may have noticed that when the president walks in, everyone in the room stands up. It is proper etiquette to stand up when a woman or someone more senior to you walks in. Opening a car door, walking on the outside of the street, saying please and thank you— manners speak volumes; just know them. Treating people with the utmost respect will only enhance the impression you make on others. For the ultimate in etiquette and manners information, go to the Emily Post Web site, http://www.bartleby.com.

5. ***Personal trainer.*** Our body is the keeper of our mind and spirit. I hate to exercise. My rule had always been, "run only when late for a plane." Last year, I made the decision to start a workout program. Within six months, my energy level had improved, as had the way I carried myself, and even how well I slept—my life was completely different. All positive. Find an exercise routine that works for you— just 15 minutes a day will make you feel great.

6. ***Presentation coach.*** Every time we walk in the door and speak to someone, we are indeed presenting. Hire an expert, not a friend. (Asking someone to critique you is a quick way to ruin a nice friendship.) Ask this person to coach you as you introduce yourself. (See the section, "Introductions," in Chapter 9.) Have him coach you when you give a presentation with slides or overheads. If you are hiring or interviewing, have someone role-play.

7. ***Acting class.*** Yes, that's acting like on stage. Find an adult
   education program that offers a short (four- to six-week)
   class. You already act now. You don't believe me? Have
   you ever talked to a baby? What happened to your voice,
   not to mention your words? Your voice pitch went up, and
   you forgot 99 percent of your vocabulary. Where did you
   learn to do that? Simple! You watched someone else talk
   to a baby, and when it was your turn, you "acted" the same
   way that person did. When you are with your kids, you act
   one way, and when you are in the office, you act another.
   Push your comfort zone. What's best is it's all for fun!
   Pay particular attention to your voice. If you spend a lot
   of time on the phone, consider taking a course in phone
   communication or radio announcing.

8. ***Business writing.*** Whether you are composing an e-mail
   or an annual report, business writing is an essential skill
   for the professional. Take a class that specifically teaches
   it—everything from style to content. For those who are
   well disciplined and can learn from a book, I suggest
   Business Writing for Dummies[3] by Sheryl Lindsell-
   Roberts.

9. ***Dentist.*** Only two-thirds of Americans have been to the
   dentist in the past 12 months, according to the Centers for
   Disease Control. Your smile and oral hygiene are crucial.
   You do not want to be remembered for your bad breath.
   There's even a Web site where you can anonymously tell
   someone they have bad breath. (*Note*: If you are ever
   offered a breath mint, take it.)

10. ***Networking coach.*** Last but certainly not least, find
    someone who can help you learn networking techniques
    and tactics. Like the others, this person needs to be
    someone you trust and to have your permission to
    help you from the outside in. She is like a symphony

conductor. On occasion, she will probably work with others on your team to find the specialist you need. Be sure you get coached both online and off. We can come across as curt online if we aren't aware of nonverbal cues. There are classes as well as online tools to help you learn how to use the social networking sites.

That's a great start! Depending on your comfort level, you may want to visit some of these providers frequently or just every so often. Once you've learned what clothing styles suit you, a refresher every year or so is worthwhile. Practice business writing and attending networking events at least once a month. The more you do, the more you learn and the more confident you are. When you have a particularly important presentation to deliver, go back to your coach. Review this list every six months to make sure you have the support network in place to ensure a successful first impression.

Skills Training

Create your own personal graduate program as you advance in your career. To stay competitive, you need skills now that you didn't need before. Many of these behaviors were not taught during your formal education—high school, college, or even graduate school. However, when these are mastered, they are the fast lane to success.

These providers take us a bit deeper inside. We have the wrapping paper all finished—we now need to add some deeper skills training.

1. ***Management training.*** It can be stressful to deal with a promotion, as you will often need to manage people who used to be your peers and balance new responsibilities. Sign up for a management course. If your firm offers one, take it. Also find something outside of the office so that you can ask questions that you may not otherwise feel

comfortable asking. Check with your human resources department for recommendations.

2. *Leadership.* Leadership training is vital for your career. There are essential, yet subtle differences between management and leadership. In some cases, people can jump from one to the other. In many situations, however, people are naturally one or the other. Learn your strengths and then place yourself in a business situation where you can excel.

3. *Sales coach.* Yes, I know that for some people, especially for nonsales professionals such as attorneys, accountants, and doctors, to name just a few, *sales* is a nasty word. However, the skills that make a great salesperson are just as important in other walks of life. Each of us must "sell" every day. Job hunters are selling their skill sets; recruiters are selling their companies; executive directors of nonprofits are selling a mission. Networking can get you to the right person; however, it doesn't end there. The transaction needs to take place.

4. *Hiring and firing skills.* If you are in a position to interview, hire, and on occasion terminate employees, have someone teach you best practices. Be sure the class includes role playing so that you can speak the words yourself, not just listen and watch someone else do it. A bad hire can be a drain on both you and the entire company—financially and otherwise.

5. *Conflict resolution and stress management.* Potential conflict is a reality when you have two or more people in an organization. Even when we are all alone, we frequently argue with ourselves.

    a. Learn the subtle but important difference between *confronting* and *confrontation.*

b. If we are able to confront people skillfully without putting them on the defensive, we are likely to avoid a confrontation.

c. Learn how to deal with differences in those you manage. Learn how different people are motivated. Realize where your buttons are, what happens when they get pushed, and how to deal with them. Understand the same about your employees.

6. *Meeting management.* As you grow in your career, you will run more meetings. Managing them well is a skill that you can easily learn. Understand ways to construct the agenda, how to "park" a topic if the discussion gets off track, conflict resolution, timing, and ways to wrap up the meeting at the end so that everyone knows what's expected next.

7. *Time and project management.* You are the keeper of your schedule, even if others plan it. Discover ways to manage your day, determine your priorities, and make time for what's most important to you, both personally and professionally. Our projects reflect our priorities as well as our organization and management skills. Study some techniques to help you process what you need to get done.

8. *Right brain/left brain.* If your job is finance, take a class in music or art. Develop an appreciation for the creative process. If you are in the creative department, take a course in business management. Learn how to read and analyze financials.

9. *Communication.* Explore communication methods—what works well for you and how to communicate effectively with those with whom you interact. Include training in negotiation skills.

10. *Career coach.* Whether you are employed or not, it is worthwhile having someone you can talk to specifically about managing your career—how to come up with a plan of action for promotion, how to handle company politics, ways to gain visibility in your industry, or how to develop a solid résumé. Check in with your coach three or four times a year, not just when you have been laid off, have been fired, or are miserable at your job.

Personal Board of Advisors

In his book *Love the Work You're With*,[4] author Richard Whiteley discusses the concept of a personal board of advisors. Companies, universities, and nonprofits have a board of advisors, why not you? These boards provide wisdom, introductions, and resources to the groups they serve. Why not have a board that does the same for you? Put together a team of five or six individuals whom you like, know, and trust.

Whiteley's book identifies six key members of your board of advisors:

1. *Politician or mentor.* Mentor was a friend of Odysseus who was entrusted with the education of Odysseus' son Telemachus. Begin exploring a relationship with someone who genuinely wants to see you succeed and has the interest and time to mentor you.

2. *Strategist.* This person looks into the future to see what you will need and helps you create a map to get you there.

3. *Problem solver.* This person focuses on the present. He has experience with implementing techniques for getting past issues and moving on to the next step.

4. *Coach.* A championship team has one, so why not you? In fact, sports teams have defensive coaches, offensive coaches, and special teams coaches. Depending on where

you are in your life, identify what is holding you back. It may not be what you or others think.

5. ***Butt kicker.*** This person doesn't let you get away with anything. If you say you can't, your butt kicker will challenge you. Be prepared—this person will take you on an adventure.

6. ***Cheerleader.*** Whitely discusses the toxicity of negative criticism. One evening while I was hosting a networking party, a friend walked up to me and said, "You look tired." I wasn't sure what the value or purpose of that comment was, and I still don't know. Your cheerleader is not a Pollyanna, but she is a positive person who sees the glass as half full rather than half empty.

Discuss with the members of your board what your expectations are. What is the time commitment you'd like from them? The more clearly defined this is, the better for all concerned. Consider putting the desired results on paper. Here are some examples:

- Within six months, I want to raise $1 million in venture money.

- By the end of the year, I want to be on track to make partner, and that means bringing in three clients with billings of $50,000 each.

- I want to find a new job in the biotech industry within the next four months.

- In the next six to nine months, I want to be promoted to a position of greater authority at another company.

How long do you see this board being active? For example, if you are moving into a new industry, you may want to identify someone who also made a transition into that industry and ask him to be available for the first 90 days of your new job. If you are making the switch from for profit to nonprofit, find someone else who made the same decision.

Determine the "term limits" for your board members. This is important both for you and for them. Decide what should happen if the relationship just isn't meeting your needs or if someone isn't comfortable with her role. What will you do? I'd caution you against holding meetings with your entire personal advisory board. I find that while these conversations can be inspiring and refreshing, at times they can be a bit draining. In most cases, you are seeking the members' individual, not collective, advice. Create a system that works for you.

Peer Group

Whether you are at the pinnacle of your career or just starting out, create a peer group. Do this outside of your company. For example, if you are head of marketing or engineering, find others who are in the same position. This group can be invaluable in your life. You can discuss topics that you wouldn't discuss with your management team, your board, your advisors, your investors, or your colleagues.

Here are some guidelines to consider for this forum:

- Rotate facilitators or have an outside one.
- Determine an agenda ahead of time and distribute it.
- Meet on a regular basis—maybe once or twice a month.
- Start with a six-month commitment from everyone.
- Define your expectations.
- Set confidentiality levels.
- Decide what constitutes a competitor.
- Determine how leads, referrals, and finder's fees will be handled.
- Write out a conflict resolution procedure and get agreement on it. If this is difficult, it will tell you something!

- Determine the requirements for participation and what to do if someone wishes to leave.
- Designate a timekeeper and a note taker.
- Create an online forum to facilitate communication between meetings. Group members can elect to receive e-mail digests of posts to the forum; it can also host materials (draft presentations, etc) for commentary and/or edits.
- Keep it to a manageable size—I suggest no larger than 12.

Networking Buddies

The first time I went scuba diving, I was terrified. I was loaded down with the weight of the world and plopped into the water, and I started sinking. What made the entire experience less threatening was my scuba buddy. A person I had never met before in my life shared an interest with me. Before we literally jumped overboard, he shared how nervous he had been on his first dive. As I somersaulted underwater, I righted myself and discovered that the dive master was holding my hand. After a quick squeeze of the hand and a thumbs-up signal, I began to enjoy the warm, clear waters and a spectacular world that I had yet to discover.

It can be frightening when you start to learn something new. Find a buddy, especially when you are attending networking forums. Some research says that the fear of walking into a room full of strangers is greater than the fear of public speaking (which is typically listed as people's number one fear).

Have more than one buddy. You can have several for different situations. When you review your network for potential buddies, here are some things to consider:

- Select someone who serves the same customers as you do but isn't a competitor. For example, you are an attorney, and your buddy works for an accounting firm that serves your same target client.

- Find someone who likes the same time frame you do—morning or evening.
- Choose someone that you trust completely.

A profile of your networking buddy is given in Figure 4-2.

The value of having a buddy depends on what you invest. This person is representing you in your shared professional circles. It is imperative that you spend time with each other so that you can intelligently answer questions and articulate what is wonderful about your buddy and vice versa. Here are some thoughts:

- Practice each other's introduction.
- Know about each other's achievements, especially recent ones.
- Determine your goals before the event.
- Agree who is responsible for the pre-event preparation. (See the section "'Whether Reports'" later in this chapter.)
- Review your buddy's snapshot. (See the section "Networking Snapshots," at the end of this chapter.)
- If possible, arrive together.
- At the check-in table, introduce yourself to at least one person and introduce your buddy.
- If you haven't eaten, have a bite together.
- Then, you *must* split up.
- One person walks clockwise and talks with people; the other works the room counterclockwise.
- Agree to meet at a specific time at a certain place *at* the event (for example, the bar at the far side of the room).
- Determine whether staying at the event is worthwhile.
- If it makes sense to stay, loop back toward the front door.
- If not, call it a night and head home!

Networking Buddy Profile

Name   _____

Title   _____

Company   _____

Direct   _____

Mobile   _____

E-mail   _____

Facebook   _____

LinkedIn   _____

Twitter   _____

Web   _____

_____

Industry   _____

Professional association memberships

_____

_____

Years in business   _____

Board positions   _____

_____

What are networking goals?

_____

_____

_____

_____

Ability to meet at networking events?

                             Morning

                             Lunch

                             After work

                             Weekends

Hours per week buddy wants to network: _____

Time unavailable   _____

Networking pet peeve(s)   _____

Figure 4-2   Networking Buddy Profile

What my buddy does:

_____

_____

_____

Target industries are:

_____

_____

_____

Target clients:

_____

_____

_____

Present clients:

_____

_____

_____

Education:

_____

_____

_____

Professional associations:

_____

_____

_____

Board positions (past and present):

_____

_____

_____

Phone: 888-907-0900   © 2010 Effective Networking, Inc.
E-mail: Info@EffectiveNetworking.com   p. 2/2

Figure 4-2   Networking Buddy Profile (*continued*)

Qualities for Everyone in Your Support Network

You do not necessarily want clones of yourself. With them, little would get accomplished. For example, if you are a CEO, you want people around you who can make sure that the day-to-day operations of the business get done while you focus on long-term strategy. If everyone looked after the long-term plan, the business would suffer in the short term and potentially fail. Choose people who have skills that are complementary to yours. If you are a vision person, find someone who loves looking at the present operation and how it affects the profitability of the business.

As you identify people that belong in your support network, here are some things to ask yourself to ensure an effective partnership. Some are more easily determined than others. If all else fails, trust your gut. Be clear with yourself on what is acceptable and unacceptable behavior. Personally, I don't feel comfortable with people who have a temper. They intimidate me and make me shut down. Typically, I arrive a few minutes before an event begins, which is frustrating for some people. If I know that promptness is an important attribute, I will be aware of my behavior and plan differently.

We all have our strengths and weaknesses. Ask yourself:

- Does this person fit in with the others?
- Does she offer pertinent knowledge?
- Do you trust this person?
- Are you compatible?
- At the end of a session with her, do you feel energized or drained?

After you run through your list of criteria a few times, you will be able to determine if there is a mutually beneficial reason for you to move forward and begin to work together.

"WHETHER REPORTS"

These will help you to decide whether or not to attend an event, join an organization, or contact someone. Some of this will also depend on your attitude and latitude at the moment. You're going to create several "whether reports." For an event "Whether Report," see Figure 4-3.

Go to www.BestPlacesToNetwork.com to see if there are reviews of the organization or event. See if there's someone you know who has been to the organization before. Give him a call and see if it's a match for you. You are a customer, and you should find out information before you purchase a ticket. Details to look for ahead of time include

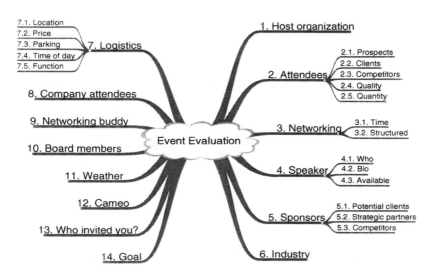

Figure 4-3 Event "Whether Report"

1. *Host organization.* Find out about the company, association, or organization and whether your missions and values are aligned.

   a. Who is the host organization?

   b. Have you attended this organization's events before?

   c. Do you know someone at the organization who can introduce you to others? Social networking sites like LinkedIn and Facebook can help here. Do a quick search for the organization or company name on LinkedIn to see a list of individuals connected to it that are also connected to you in some way. If you are connected through a mutual acquaintance, see if that person can provide an introduction prior to the event. If the organization has a Facebook page, it will often contain useful information and ideas for conversational "hooks." An individual's Facebook profile can provide insights into her interests outside the workplace, some of which you may share.

2. *Attendees.*

   a. Who will be attending, and why are they there? Again, if time permits, you can try to find them on LinkedIn or Facebook.

   b. If they are prospects, invite them to join you. These would also be good candidates for a pre-event introduction via LinkedIn.

   c. If they are clients, be sure that someone on your team greets them and makes a connection. If you do not, you can be sure that your competition will.

   d. Will your competitors be attending? Or are they perhaps sponsoring the event?

   e. What level are the attendees? Do they make decisions about purchasing your product or service?

f. How many people will be at the event? In some cases, smaller events are much better. You have a greater opportunity to connect with the attendees.

3. ***Networking.*** In many cases, it's the time with the other attendees that determines the value of the event. Don't cross an event off your "whether report" list just because time is not specifically allotted to networking, however, if the event is germane to your professional or personal interests. For example, there is an event that I attend every year. I like to go because the speakers are excellent, even though there isn't any time for networking. In addition, even in the most overscheduled of events, there is always the opportunity to meet someone interesting with whom you can meet later!

a. How much time is allowed for networking? Is it before the event/speaker? After? Both? Be sure there is time to meet the attendees. You may be surprised, but this isn't always the case.

b. How is the networking set up? Are there separate rooms for sponsors, vendors, and clients? Is the networking facilitated? At some meetings, there is someone who keeps the introductions going and has an eye on the time.

4. ***Speaker.*** This individual often drives the event.

a. Who is the speaker? Is she qualified to speak on the topic? Is she someone that you would like to meet? If so, why? Do you have common acquaintances? (LinkedIn can help here.)

b. Check out the speaker's bio, which is typically available on the event Web site.

c. Will the speaker be available to meet with the audience after her presentation? In some cases, the answer is yes. In many cases, however, the speaker is swept away, and you do not have any access to her. This is one reason I like to get to events early. Before the presentation is often a great time to chat with the speaker—plus you get to make your impression before the crowd that will be vying for her attention after the presentation.

5. *Sponsors.* Find out who the sponsors will be. This is another opportunity to make a connection or get some strategic information. Are any of them:
   a. Potential clients
   b. Strategic partners
   c. Competitors

6. *Industry.*
   a. Is the purpose of the event related to your industry?
   b. Is it designed to educate those who are employed in the market?
   c. Consider attending an event that is outside your industry.

7. *Logistics.* These factors can make or break your decision.
   a. *Location.* Is the event easy to get to from your office?
   b. *Price.* Is it worth the money? Expensive events can be worth every penny if there are people there that you do not have the opportunity to meet otherwise. Free events can be very expensive if you are trapped with an audience or speaker that is a mismatch for your goals. Consider other expenses as well: travel, lodging, clothing, and so on.
   c. *Parking.* Some cities are more conducive to transportation than others. If you are going by car, know the costs and availability of parking and make allowances for the time required to park!

d. *Time of day.* Different opportunities exist at morning and evening events. Know the schedule and the goal of the gathering.

       i. For some people, the morning is best. Others can't possibly leave the house early because of family responsibilities.

      ii. Know what you can and cannot do without risking your other obligations.

     iii. Remember, networking doesn't just take place at the office.

    e. *Function.* What type of event is it? This determines your preparation including clothing. Do you need to bring a gift or any other special considerations?

8. **Company attendees.**

    a. Who from your office will attend?

    b. Is he the best representative?

    c. Is he comfortable explaining your product or service?

9. **Networking buddy.**

    a. If this is the first time you have attended an event with this organization, try to find a buddy to go with you. Refer to the previous discussion about developing a "pool" of buddies.

    b. Determine which buddy is best.

    c. Practice each other's introductions prior to the event.

10. **Board members.**

    a. Do you know any of the board members of the organization?

    b. Are any of them prospects or clients?

    c. E-mail them ahead of time so that they know to look out for you.

11. **Weather.**

   a. This category can work for you either way.

   b. If it's a nice day, people will not want to be inside.

   c. However, if it's raining or snowing, they may not venture out of their office.

   d. Determine what works for you. Remember, safety always comes first.

12. **Cameo.** This is when you make a quick appearance, then leave.

   a. If you must do this because of scheduling, let the host know in advance. If you cannot stay for the entire event, find someone from your company who can.

13. **Who invited you?**

   a. In many cases, this determines whether or not people attend an event. If the invitation was extended by someone of importance, they are more likely to attend.

14. **Goal.**

   a. Do you know why you are attending the event?

   b. What do you hope to accomplish?

   c. When you leave, how will you judge whether it was a success or not?

An organization "whether report" helps you determine whether or not to participate in the organization. (See Figure 4-4.) Just review a few of these questions as you consider whether or not to participate in an organization:

1. Do you feel welcome when you arrive?

2. Are the attendees in your industry?

3. Are the attendees decision makers?

4. What time of day are the events or meetings? Does that work with your schedule?

5. Who is on the board?

6. Is there an opportunity for you to add value to the organization? It can be frustrating if you don't have a chance to contribute.

7. Am I looking forward to the event? It's hard to have fun if you're dreading a gathering. Some are obligatory (conference or sadly a memorial service). Sometimes that is the reality of being a grown-up.

8. What is your goal for joining?

A contact "whether report" helps you determine whether or not to contact someone. (See Figure 4-5.) It is worthwhile reviewing these questions before you make contact. In some cases, you may realize that this person has already given you advice.

Figure 4-4   Organization "Whether Report"

Figure 4-5   Contact "Whether Report"

1. How do you know the person you are calling?
2. Who introduced you? What is the person up to?
3. When was the last time you spoke to the person? Have you asked the person for advice?
4. Did you take her advice then?
5. What are you asking for?
6. Have you written it down and practiced saying it out loud?
7. Are you prepared to hear yes?
8. Are you prepared to hear no?

HOW TO QUALIFY A NETWORKING EVENT

Given the demands on our time, if we are to be away from the office or our family, networking needs to be worthwhile. It's hard to determine the value of an opportunity if we have not attended an event hosted by an organization before or if the organization is new to us. In addition to the "whether reports," ask yourself why you are going to the event. I recommend that you organize your reasons into three main categories:

1. Connecting with colleagues
2. Business opportunities
3. Personal growth

Connecting with Colleagues

An attorney at a bar association meeting will logically meet many other lawyers. Attorneys have wills, real estate purchases, and other personal transactions that require legal review. It's less likely, however, that you will win a corporate account at a meeting of a professional association that serves your profession or industry.

It is more likely that you will meet others who will be professional resources for you. They may mentor you or vice versa. If you are considering taking an active role in the organization, this is where you can meet present committee members to learn more about the commitment. In addition, you can share stories of challenges and successes in your industry and gain good contacts for future career management.

Business Opportunities

At such an event, you will see current clients and meet potential new ones. It is an ideal time to "press the flesh" and invest in some face-to-face networking. Clients like to see people with whom they do business in other settings. Make a point of introducing prospects to some of your happy clients. Find commonalities between the two—perhaps they have children at the same school, or they recently went on vacation to the same place, or they have common interests and hobbies.

Sporting events are natural for business connections. Companies have season tickets to take customers or prospects to a game. I was delighted to join four others one time to see the Boston Celtics play the Lakers. One of the reasons why golf is so popular with business professionals is that you can talk while you are playing.

Personal Growth

Professionals who want to grow their career are active learners. They attend classes, seminars, and conferences dedicated to enriching their knowledge of a subject. Typically there is time for networking at these sessions to meet both colleagues and business prospects.

Once I decided to speak at an event because it was held at the new Ritz Carlton in Boston and I wanted to see the newly renovated hotel and meet the staff.

Summary: By taking the time to prequalify an event, you significantly increase the likelihood of a successful experience.

NETWORKING SNAPSHOT

The purpose of the snapshot is to give the other person some background about you and also to share any special requests with her. This is a combination of a biography and a résumé, and it includes personal data. (See Figure 4-6.) The snapshot provides conversation starters. After someone reads it, there are a number of things she knows about you and can ask. There may be some shared interests.

Smith and Jones
123 Main Street
Anytown, Anystate, USA
Phone: 321-123-1234
Web: www.Jones.com
E-mail:Bailey@Jones.com
Facebook: www.Facebook.com/BillBailey
LinkedIn: www.LinkedIn.com/in/BillBailey
Twitter: www.Twitter:@BillBailey

Bill Bailey – Snapshot

Professional:
Partner at Smith and Jones. We help clients with all aspects of their legal needs. My expertise is mergers and acquisitions.

Previously worked for state attorney, Tiger Tank Gas Company, and Best University.

Published:
Written several articles for legal journals, including *Lawyers Monthly*.

Clients include:
Bank Three, British Express, Micronut, and Special Electric.

Residence:
Live in Anytown. Used to live in Memphis, London, Paris, and Cairo.

Family:
Married to high school sweetheart, Susan. Have two daughters, Sally (8) and Cindy (4).

Education:
Central University, South College, and North High School.

Hobbies:
Sailing, skydiving, skiing, playing chess, watching football, and reading. Former quarterback for Chicago Bears.

Associations:
President of the Any State Bar Association. Actively involved in the Anytown Rotary Club. Coach daughter's soccer team.

Best way to contact: Bailey@Jones.com

Figure 4-6   Networking Snapshot

5

Networking Accessories

There are some basic networking tools that you should have at all times. Just like the scouts, be prepared! Depending on your destination, some items may vary.

BUSINESS CARDS

Cards are a part of life. In childhood, you had baseball cards and playing cards; now you have credit cards and business cards. We feel grown up the first time we get "carded." No matter whom I ask, business cards are the number one networking must-have. Even people with sophisticated networking toys still carry and exchange business cards.

Just because you are carrying cash and credit cards doesn't mean that you are going to spend money. It does mean that you are ready in case there is something you want to buy. The same is true with business cards. Always carry them.

What Makes a Good Card

- *Basic information.* I'm amazed at how many cards I get that don't have an e-mail address or phone number. Have someone proofread your card to see if there's any crucial information missing.

- *Social networking information.* Sites like LinkedIn have emerged fairly recently, so many people don't yet have them on their cards. It can be a challenge for people to remember a Twitter handle, blog URL, or your other online contact information. I encourage people who don't have their own Web site to include their LinkedIn info, at least. For example, mine is www.LinkedIn.com/in/DianeDarling.

- *Design.* It should be clear and crisp, with good white space. It should say something about your business or about you.

- *Font.* Use a minimum of 10 point. Pick a readable font.

- *Paper quality.* Use at least an 80-pound strength and 14-point thickness.

- *Job hunters.* It isn't necessary to put your home address on the card, particularly for women. Your phone number and e-mail address are most important. (Consider getting a second phone line at home—your children or your babysitter wouldn't be answering your phone at work; why should they answer it when you are working to get a job? Or use a cell phone number if you are reachable on it in enough places and have voice mail.)

- *Home-based business.* Have a separate phone line or use your cell number. Having your adorable 6-year-old answering a business call may not send the message you want.

- *Folded cards.* These can be eye-catching; however, they are sometimes too gimmicky. They also don't fit in Rolodexes or go through card scanners. Use a folded card as a leave-behind card (discussed later in the chapter), rather than a business card.

- *Backside.* There are differing opinions here. Some feel that this should be left blank for notes; others say that it is prime real estate for explaining what you do or what your company does. If you do use the backside, consider leaving some space for the person receiving the card to write a line or two.
- ***Be sure that all information is up-to-date and that there are no typos.***

When to Hand Out a Card

- At meetings, I suggest that cards be handed out at the beginning. I put them in front of me and mirror where people are sitting around the table. It helps me remember names. (Just because it's an internal meeting doesn't mean you'll know everyone. Also if someone starts handing out cards, you don't want to be left out. Bring cards to meetings!)
- At a networking event, cards are more typically given out after a conversation.
- Don't just walk up to people at events and hand out cards.
- Give a card when it is asked for.
- Ask for a card if you want to follow up. Mention that you will be calling; the person's body language will give you an indication of how she feels about this.
- Should you give out two cards? I've seen some people do this in the hope that you will pass one on. I don't carry around other people's cards, so I toss the second one away if I'm given it.

- If you are sharing someone's contact information (e.g., a referral), write it on the back of your card and add an arrow on the front. (See Figure 5-1.)
- Always carry business cards. (Yes, I know I've said it before—but it's important, so please don't forget it.)
- Be wise about giving a card to a senior executive unless it is asked for.

Create a "Leave-Behind Card"

When I give out my business card, I also give people a different card that has networking hints. The card often leads to a discussion about

Sunshine Travel

John Jones, CEO
123 Main Street
Heartland, USA
212-555-1212
www.Facebook.com/SunshineTravel
www.LinkedIn.com/in/SunshineTravel
Twitter: @SunshineTravel
John@travel.com   →

Sally — call Kathy Smith at Smith, Snyder & Sinclair.
She can help you with your legal needs.

Figure 5-1   Sample Business Card with Referral

networking; people test their handshakes with me, and it creates a conversation.

I'd encourage you to do this. For example, if you are an accountant, have a card that provides some of the unknown tax deductions. If you represent a charity, write whom you serve and what problem you solve. If you have a product, write out some of the benefits that people experience when they use it. If you are recruiting a new hire, write out the job description.

This is very memorable, and it gives people something that they can easily find later on. (See Figure 5-2.)

Card Cases

Your business cards reflect you and your company. If they are at the bottom of your briefcase, they seem like an afterthought. If they are stuffed into your pocket, it reveals the way you think: disorganized

---

**Effective
Networking, Inc.**

Handshakes:
Two shakes, and let go!

Where to put your name badge:
On the right side of your chest (the eye naturally flows up the right arm as you are shaking hands).

How long to talk to one person:
Three to five minutes, eight minutes maximum.

Networking wardrobe:
When in doubt, go up a notch.

Take a networking kit:
A pen that you can lose, a Sharpie—to embolden your name on the name badge, breath mints, and business cards in a case.

What to talk about:
First, have a prepared tagline—what you're going to say after your name. Also come armed with three neutral questions, for example, are you from the area?

What not to talk about:
Personal stuff, sex, religion, and politics.

Eating:
Do not arrive hungry. It's difficult to juggle food with handshaking and business card exchanges. This is network, not net-eat.

Drinking:
Always keep your drink in your left hand. Otherwise your handshake will feel clammy.

Thank-you notes:
How many handwritten notes do you get a day? Take an extra moment and write one. It's more noticeable than an e-mail.

Figure 5-2 Leave-Behind Card

and haphazard. Respect your cards and put them in a case. They are your image when you are not around. Show others that you take care of them. Here are some ways to send a positive message.

- Carry two cases, one for your cards and the other for cards you receive.
- Inventory your case before and after each event.
- Resupply as needed.

Business Card Management

Finding someone's contact information when you want it, and quickly, is what matters. You can have the best and largest collection of cards in the world, but if you cannot find the one you need, it's just an exercise in frustration, and you feel as if you are drowning in business card clutter. Find a system that works for you. Be patient; in all likelihood, it will change a few times.

There are several phases of business card management. They include:

- *Processing cards.* What you do with them when you get them
- *Storage and retrieval.* How you keep them and how you find your contacts when you want to

Here are some tested ideas, suggestions, and products that I'm happy to share with you:

1. *Processing cards.*
   a. Start from the moment you receive the card. The process begins here.
   b. Your right-hand pocket is for your cards (outbound); your left-hand pocket is for other people's cards (inbound).
   c. You shake hands with your right hand, so it's natural for you to give your card with your right hand.

d. *Look at the card when you receive it.* Make a connection between the person and the card. Notice the color and design. Ask a question about the location—e.g., "I've always wanted to try the Italian restaurant on the corner. Is it good?"

e. *Have separate card cases.* Then there will never be a chance that you will hand out someone else's card instead of your own.

f. *Immediately put the inbound cards into a container.* My very high-tech way of organizing cards is called ziplock bags. I have small ones, and I write the name of the event, date, and any other details on the bag. We have all had the experience of finding a business card tucked in a corner of our wallet or a very safe pocket in our briefcase, only to say, "Oh, that's where that card is."

g. *Make a note of something on someone's card that you owe the person so that you can follow up.* Except when you are dealing with Japanese, it's okay to write on someone's card in front of him.

h. *Screen and sort the cards:*

   i. When you return from a networking event, take a few minutes and review the cards while the names are fresh in your mind.

   ii. Write on the back of each card what you promised the person you would do. Be sure to do what you said you would do within five to seven days maximum. In some cases, note something memorable (discussed sailing, wearing bright pink, wants to travel to Thailand).

   iii. Sort cards by priority of how quickly you need to follow up. I have one master database. This is difficult to do, but I encourage you to try to have one main location for all your contact points.

iv. Determine which cards you want to keep –(for the most part, I keep them all). The extent or relevance of your conversation will help you decide this. This becomes the "net" rather than the gross of whom you met. In this process, you are determining in which network they belong.

    a. Some things to consider in general are

        i. Did I like the person?

        ii. Will I be able to add value to the person's business in the future?

        iii. Will the person be able to help me?

        iv. Does the person belong on my mailing list?

Go to www.EffectiveNetworking.com and click on Products for business card systems that will be helpful.

    i. *Convert the cards to a database for storage.*

        i. Determine which database works for you. Given that we are now a mobile society, it is likely that you want something that can interface with your mobile device. Online databases are popular because the information is available whenever you have Web access. Storage capacity is less of an issue.

        ii. Scanners. A business card scanner does what its name describes: it scans business cards and then transfers them into a variety of software programs. It is quite accurate. It is especially useful when you return from a conference and have a large number of cards. It does not work for folded cards.

        iii. Data entry is your other choice. This is something I do while I'm watching a sitcom or some other TV show where my full attention is not required.

2. *Storage and retrieval.* Try different systems, ask others what they do, and be patient with yourself. No one I've

How I Prioritize Business Cards

I split the cards I receive into three groups: A, B, and C.

A. This is my "action" list. This follow-up can be done very quickly, and if you're lucky enough to have an assistant, he can help you. These are people to whom I owe information; maybe it's a restaurant, a Web site, or an introduction to a person. Often this can be done by e-mail or via one of the social networking sites.

B. This is my "let's have a cup of coffee" list. I *rarely* ask someone for lunch. It can be a *long* and boring waste of time. And with true proper etiquette, if you invite, you pay. Coffee is less expensive. I ask someone for a 20-minute meeting, suggest a few dates and times, and offer to bring their favorite coffee to them.

C. This is my "whenever if ever" list. Even if the conversation hasn't been particularly productive or there is not a clear next action step, I still put the person's information into the system.

Should you keep or toss business cards? People have their own opinions on this—I'll say do what works for you. I've devised the perfect system for me (mind you, that doesn't always mean that I do it!). Here's my system:

- Cards go into the ziplock.
- Cards get entered into the database.
- Follow-up is done according to the A, B, C model noted earlier.
- A and B cards are moved from the event ziplock into an A or B bag. That becomes a physical tickler file for me as well as the database.

met so far is genuinely satisfied with her method. Here are some techniques I use:

a. *Categorize your contacts as you input your cards.* This simple task will significantly help you later when you need to retrieve cards. If the time this takes seems frustrating, imagine yourself on the other end when you are seeking a card and you can't find it. Please go to www. EffectiveNetworking.com/Resources for sample downloads to help you manage your data.

i. Sample categories or groups are *mailing list, vendor, alumni friends*, and *colleagues*. You can also use industry, such as *financial services* or *technology*. I use an online database to manage my names, and as I was working on this book, I created a group called NSG. This was a list of people who wanted to be notified when *The Networking Survival Guide* was available.

ii. User fields can be customized, and I would encourage you to do so. Here are a few fields you may want to create.

- *Met date.* Most databases have a birthday field. I use this for the day I met the person.
- *Met where.* This is where I put in the location, organization, or person who introduced us.
- *Next steps.* This helps you track your to-dos.

iii. Business card sheets. What is good about this storage method is that you can see each card. This is good because many of us remember people when we look at their card. Also, the sheets can be stored in three-ring binders. These can hold 10 business cards on each side. Because I write on the back of many cards, I don't use the back side of the sheet, so this method can get expensive quickly. Or place the cards on the copier, 3-hole punch the sheet, file and toss the cards.

iv. Rolodex. This is one of the classic ways to keep cards. If it works for you, do it!

v. Rubber bands. This is the storage system I most frequently find people using. It appears to be fast; however, it can quickly be deceiving. Trying to find a card can take a long time. If this works for you, use it. If this is the only place you have the data, be careful, since sometimes these stacks can get lost.

Summary: There are a number of ways to manage your cards—by last name, by company, by the event where you met, by type of vendor, or by some other category. You can use software, Rolodex, or even rubber bands. Use what works for you and your company.

MOBILE DEVICES—TO BUMP OR NOT TO BUMP

With the plethora of technology toys, the question arises: Do we use them to share our business info or not?

Mobile toys have the ability to swap information without the hassle of exchanging business cards. It's not trading the cards that's the hassle, of course; it's entering the data, filing the cards, and, most important, being able to retrieve the right card when we need to.

While researching this book, I discovered that most people like to get the physical card, even if contact info is exchanged electronically. They like it as a visual reminder and a tickler.

One time when I was sharing information, I received not only the person's name and contact information, but also some passwords and credit card numbers. After I went shopping at Amazon, I called and let him know. (Just kidding!) Bumpers beware!

I asked several entrepreneurs who specialize in creating products for mobile devices, why not develop a "basket" to catch all the cards from a specific networking event? For example, ask the device to find all cards gathered between 7 and 10 a.m. on March 2, 2010. If you know of someone who can make this product, please contact us.

Summary: Have paper business cards, and carry them at all times. Be careful when you beam or share your information electronically.

NOTEPAD AND PEN

A few years ago, someone asked me to lunch and said that he wanted some ideas on the travel business. I was happy to help. During the course of the conversation, I started giving him ideas and names of people who could help him. After a few minutes, I realized that he was not taking any notes—in fact, he didn't even *have* a piece of paper or a pen.

When someone is sharing information, be *prepared* to write notes. Ask permission first. It is unrealistic to expect that you will remember names, phone numbers, and e-mails, not to mention the ideas that this person is sharing. It's disrespectful to ask for someone's time and then not value the information that is shared.

The notepad, notebook or portfolio should be clean and simple. Get something classic and functional. Pull out a *clean* sheet of paper. The person would not be taking his time to share valuable information with you if you were not important to him. Treat the person with respect and send the signal that you value the information by using proper paper.

Always carry a pen. Make sure that the pen works. Personally I would suggest one of three choices:

- *A classic pen:* Mont Blanc, Cross, Schaeffer, and so on
- *A pen that is a conversation piece:* antique, family pen, and so on
- A pen that you can lose and that is not chewed. If you are hungry, get some food.

Would you go out of the house without your shoes and socks? Professionally, that is what you are doing when you are without pen and paper. Think back to the toes example—this may seem small, but it's an expression of you. You will fall flat on your face if you don't have the information you need. Like everything else, it either reinforces your personal brand or sends a conflicting message. If you act as if you don't appreciate the information you are being given, people won't take the time to help you.

Summary: Be prepared!

BRIEFCASE

This is an extension of your image. Maximize the opportunity by owning a classy bag that complements your look. Personally, I like briefcases that are very easy to open; have some pockets, but not too many; and are well made.

Here are some things to keep in mind when you go briefcase shopping:

- *Weight.* How much weight do you want to carry? Some bags quickly get heavy.
- *Classic or funky.* Funky can get tiring fast. Functional is better.
- *Leather or nylon.* If you travel in areas where it frequently rains, consider a nylon bag.
- *Entry.* Can you open the case with one hand and keep your eye on the person with whom you are speaking?

THINGS THAT BEEP

Mobile devices are a part of our lives. Sometimes they are very useful tools that facilitate and streamline communication. Other times they are a nuisance and can have a very negative impact on those around you. Whenever there is a ring, you have a choice. At that moment, your actions indicate your priorities—who is more important, the person you are speaking with or the person who is calling. It's decision time. Your decision reflects on your personal brand. It tells the other person who is more important.

We have all experienced the awkward feeling of finding ourselves part of a conversation that we really don't want to be in the middle of, such as an argument between work colleagues or business negotiations that are less than pleasant. Not only is this unprofessional, but it can also be detrimental to your success. A story was shared with me about someone on a commuter train who was using a cell phone to complain about someone he worked with. Another person from the firm was also on the train, and the overheard conversation was reported to human resources and quickly derailed the individual's career at that firm.

As with any other form of technology, it isn't the object itself but how we use it that matters. Consider your surroundings and determine what's best. This means that you understand and respect the fact that cell phone conversations are public and that the exchange may not be one that should be broadcast.

If you cannot manage your technology, you are sending the signal that you may not be able to manage a project or a new job, or that you may not use a contribution to a nonprofit wisely. This is a negative signal that can sabotage the likelihood that you and the other person will work together. Here are some pointers:

- If you are expecting a call that cannot be missed, tell the other person. This is less annoying to someone you are meeting with if you are up-front and honest about it. Let the person know the circumstances ahead of time, and apologize in advance that your meeting may be interrupted. Speak briefly and hang up right away, and then turn off your phone.

- Ring volume can downright take your breath away! I've nearly jumped out of my skin when someone's phone went off. Invest a few minutes of time in getting to know your phone and where the buttons are—especially the volume.
- Most phones come with a variety of clever rings. Find one that is distinctive to you, but not utterly annoying. Yes, the attention can be fun; however, it can also make you look quite unprofessional.
- Turn your phone to vibrate or silent.

Summary: If you are able to manage your technology, you are sending the message that you are able to manage other things in your life. That's a positive message to send and one that is appreciated by many.

6

Body Language, Voice, and Words

It's important that you choose the most appropriate communication method for a given situation. For example, sending someone an e-mail or a text isn't the best way to tell him that he no longer has a job. At the same time, you don't need to be face-to-face to give someone directions when a link to a map will do.

What you have to say determines *how* you should say it.

When we speak in person, we communicate in three ways: with our words, our tone, and our body language. Professor Albert Mehrabian of UCLA researched these carefully, and found that our words account for only 7 percent of our communication power. We communicate 55 percent using our body language and 38 percent using our voice, tone, and pitch![1] (See Figure 6-1.)

Maybe this is where the phrase "actions speak louder than words" came from. Even plastic surgeons have noted the impact that body language can have on someone's career. When asked to identify good candidates for Botox, they list "executives, attorneys, and salesmen."[2]

In an article in the *San Francisco Chronicle*, the author noted, "Politicians, trial attorneys and others whose livelihoods depend on

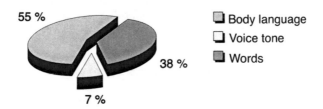

Figure 6-1   Body Language, Voice, and Words
(Source: "Decoding Inconsistent Communication," Prof. Albert Mehrabian, UCLA.)

a deadpan expression will be able to realize great gains over their un-Botox-enhanced fellows."[3]

When you are online, you may be forfeiting as much as 93 percent of your communication power. Misunderstandings have become far more common in the age of e-mail and text messaging. While methods have emerged to convey tone (smileys, anyone?), these are not generally appropriate in business communications. Recommendation: save that sardonic wit for an in-person meeting!

BODY LANGUAGE

Given what we now know about the power of body language, note the impact of body language on the "mood" of the image.

Here are some guidelines:

- Have at least 18 inches of personal space around you when you talk to others.
- Do not slouch. Shoulders should not be confused with earrings.
- Keep shoulders and hips parallel.

- Smile!
- Maintain good eye contact without staring.
- Keep your hands out of your pockets.
- Do not rattle change in your pocket; this is very distracting!

These exercises illustrate how a few shifts in body language can significantly affect your experience with another person.

Exercise 1

- This requires two people and two chairs.
- Set the chairs up so that the people have their backs to each other.
- Each reads the following:

Susan: "Hello, I'm Susan Smith."
George: "Hi, Susan—I'm George Jones."
Susan: "Have you been to this meeting before?"
George: "I have. I really like the group. I take it this is your first visit."
Susan: "I attended a session a few months ago, and then I got busy. What do you do?"
George: "I help manage companies. Right now I'm with a pharmaceutical company, and we create drugs that reduce fever in children."

Now stop.

- What did talking with your backs to each other feel like?
- Did you feel that the other person was listening?
- Did you feel that the other person was interested in continuing the conversation or in stopping as soon as possible?

Exercise 2

- Turn your chairs around, sit down, and face each other.
- Repeat the same dialogue.

Let's review:

- How did it feel?
- Was it different when you were facing each other?
- Discuss what felt different.

Exercise 3

- Now stand up and move the chairs out of the way.
- Stand a few feet apart as if you were at a cocktail party.
- Cross your arms and avoid eye contact.
- Repeat the same dialogue.

Please review:

- Describe how it felt.
- You become more engaged in the dialogue when you are standing.
- Also, you tend to pay closer attention when you are speaking.

Exercise 4

- Stay standing.
- Drop your arms to your sides.
- Reach out and shake hands.
- Look each other straight in the eye when you say your name.
- Repeat the same dialogue.

As your body language shifts, so do your attention and your commitment to the conversation. When you are speaking with someone, face toward her as much as feels comfortable. This may feel a bit intimidating in the beginning; however, the more you practice, the better it will feel. When your arms are across your body, this is an unfriendly signal—you are guarding your heart and chest area.

It takes practice and calm confidence to feel open and safe while engaging in a conversation with someone you don't know.

Summary: Given how much you "say" with your body language it is important to learn and practice techniques that will help you express yourself.

VOICE AND TONE

In the film *Three Men and a Baby*, there is a scene in which Tom Selleck's character is reading to the baby. His voice sounds like he is reading a children's story. When challenged by his roommates, he points out that it doesn't matter that he is reading the sports section of the newspaper; what is important is his tone of voice.

Question or Answer—Inflection

Listen to people talk. It's curious how many sound as if they are asking questions when in fact they are making statements. It even happens when you first meet someone.

Do you make a statement or ask a question? "I'm Diane Darling?" Aren't you really sure? This isn't a question—this is a true statement.

Practice saying your name as a statement.

Do it again. Now a third time. Hear the difference?

Now add an additional sentence about what you do. For example, "Effective Networking helps organizations create 'people' networking plans and helps people refine their networking skills."

Again, this is a statement. I've heard people say "I'm a VP of marketing?" with their voice going up at the end. Aren't you sure you are? Why raise doubt? If you don't believe you are the VP, why should anyone else?

Now put it all together. "I'm Diane Darling from Effective Networking. We help organizations create 'people' networking plans and help people feel confident when they network."

Is Your Voice Smiling?

When you talk to someone on the phone, you can hear him smile. His voice has energy, enthusiasm, and a sense of purpose. The next time the phone rings, smile before you answer it. Consider standing up. That call is important. When we hear a content voice, we feel calm and assured that we are dealing with a friendly professional.

On the other hand, if the other person is speaking fast and seems agitated, the feeling is just the opposite. "Please don't bother me," this says. We've all heard the angry voice. Take the time to tape yourself. I don't know anyone who really likes her voice; however, it's what you have. Learn some techniques to help maximize your communication power.

It isn't clear where the word *phony* came from. The dictionary suggests that it came from a brass ringing sound in an Irish "confidence" game. Others say that it came from the word *phone*. Does your tone of voice sound genuine or lacking in confidence? Do you come across as if you really are interested in the conversation you are having?

Take charge of the pace. If someone is anxious, slow your speech down. If the conversation is dragging, pick up the pace.

Don't mumble or talk too softly. Most people don't read lips and do want to hear what you have to say. Talk at a pitch and volume that are appropriate for your setting. Find a voice buddy at work who frequently hears you on the phone. Let him know that you are working on improving your voice skills and ask for his assistance.

Summary: Given that you now know that your nonverbal skills are so important, take the time to stretch your skills and learn new techniques.

WORDS

If you look at a brick building, you will see that the cement holding the building together is much smaller than the bricks; however, it keeps the structure from falling over. Your words are the same. When we talk with someone who doesn't speak our language, we immediately feel as if we have our hands tied behind our back.

While body language and tone of voice make up 93 percent of your communication power, you need high-quality, powerful, and carefully chosen "glue" to hold it all together. This is where your words come in. Here are some thoughts:

- Select a vocabulary level that is appropriate for the audience.
- Acronyms and industry jargon are great if everyone in the meeting knows what you mean. Otherwise, you sound as if you are talking down to people. Also, the same acronym can mean different things to different people.
- Sports analogies work if your audience is made up of fellow sports fans. If it isn't, you risk alienating your listeners.
- Refrain from using slang, vulgarities, or clichés.
- Speak in complete sentences.
- Use proper grammar.
- Get videotaped periodically and view the videotape (preferably with your presentation coach) for immediate feedback on all these topics.

Summary: For maximum networking success, be aware of all three aspects: body language, voice/tone, and your words. Consider this: when we send an e-mail, we forfeit 93 percent of our communication power!

7

Conversations

When you have a taste for exceptional people, you always
end up meeting them everywhere.

~ MAC ORLAN

At the heart and soul of any networking interaction is a conversation. When people share stories, interests, and ideas, they build rapport. When a connection is established, people want to continue to listen. In business, it is essential to get someone's attention first in order to continue and potentially do business together. How you are perceived in a discussion affects how you will be judged professionally.

Good conversation helps you win on two levels:

1. It strengthens your self-confidence (a trait that others want to see).
2. It makes you memorable.

The advance research we talked about earlier in the book can be incredibly valuable in fueling your conversations. Mutual acquaintances or shared interests can fill the void that can occur after the initial information is exchanged. It's far easier to be confident if you already have a list of things to talk about. These are in addition to the context-related conversational items—the meeting, the facility, and so on. Your ability to move beyond these will help you to be more memorable.

CONVERSATION STARTERS

There are two types of people. Those who come into a room and say, "Well, here I am!" and those who come in and say, "Ah, there you are."

~ FREDERICK L. COLLINS

Here are some ways to start conversations.

- *Prior to the event, prepare three neutral questions that you can ask.* Here are examples:
  - Tell me how you know the host, the company, and so on.
  - What made you decide to come to this event?
  - What other organizations in the _____ industry do you belong to?
- *Focus on neutral topics.* Here's a list:
  - Have you ever been to one of these events before?
  - Is the location near your home?
  - The latest news on the local sports team
  - Be observant—what is around you? A special attraction, park, or something similar?
  - What business you are in
  - Movies
  - Books
  - Sports you play
- *Replenish your conversation starter repertoire.* Here are some ways:
  - Read the newspaper. Just skim the headlines and top stories. This can take as little as 15 minutes.

- ○ Watch national and local news.
- ○ Look at three types of magazine covers: news (*Time* or *Newsweek*), business (*BusinessWeek, Fortune,* or *Forbes*), and general interest (*People*). Each cover is a conversation starter.
- ○ Know what's happening in the business world even if you don't work in it. This affects you directly or indirectly and is often a conversation starter.
- ○ Know about the latest sports news, particularly about how your home team is doing—the same is true with sports.

- *Begin with a smile, eye contact, and an outstretched hand.*
- *It doesn't need to cover every subject possible.* This is the beginning.
- *Make it simple!*
- *Comment on a man's tie, or a woman's earrings, scarf, or pin.* Stay with neutral comments to build rapport so that you won't be accused of flirting or sexual harassment—"I'd like to get something like that for my brother or sister."
- *If you are feeling nervous, you are thinking too much about yourself.* This is about making the *other* person feel important.

SMALL TALK

Effective questioning brings insight, which fuels curiosity, which cultivates wisdom.

~ CHIP BELL

I often hear, I don't like small talk. It's usually a brilliant person telling me this. There's not way to prove that smart people dislike small talk and not-so-smart people do. However meaningful conversations typically start with small talk. Some people undervalue this exchange as being mindless and an evil necessity. Think of the start of a dialogue as first gear in your car. While you may get going if you start in third or fourth gear, it isn't typically a pleasant way to start. You lurch forward and perhaps stall. Keep the following in mind while you cruise through the lower gears of conversation:

- Ask open-ended questions, then shut up and listen.
- Don't just talk about yourself.
- Participate in the discussion—don't wait for someone else to initiate it.
- Don't answer questions with just one or two words.
- Lead the conversation to a new topic if the present one is getting inappropriate or not going anywhere.
- Compliment someone on his attire or a recent accomplishment.

SOME GUIDELINES FOR GOOD CONVERSATIONS

For some people, conversation comes easily. For others, it feels like a dreaded chore. Like anything else, this takes practice. Conversations are a part of life, and the more you try, the better you will become. Before too long, others will ask you to teach them. Here are some guidelines:

- Listen. You were given two ears and one mouth; take the hint!
- Don't be afraid to laugh, especially at yourself.
- Be aware of your body language and pay attention to the other person's.
- Be sincerely interested in others.
- Find commonalities.
- Remember that "thank you" and "please" are your two golden keys.
- Respect the other person's views.
- Remember that everyone's ego is fragile.

- Engage those around you.
- Don't interrupt.
- Don't finish other people's sentences.
- Don't control the conversation.
- Include others.

WHEN TO BREAK INTO A CONVERSATION

This is one of the more challenging and intimidating moments—when you walk in and there are conversations in progress. Others are participating, and you want to join, but how? Here are some thoughts:

- When there are just two people, I don't recommend breaking in.
- When there are three or more, it's fine.
- Catch the eye of one of the group members.
- Smile as you walk up.
- Offer your hand.
- Introduce yourself and explain how you fit into the event, for example, "I'm Diane Darling, and this is my first visit to the Mickey Mouse Club. Minnie invited me."
- Ask a question, such as, "How long have each of you been members?"

CONVERSATION TOPICS TO BE WARY OF

Here is a list of topics that *can* be delicate. This doesn't mean that you always need to steer away from them. But you need to approach them gently and cautiously. Be prepared to switch topics if the conversation gets contentious or if damage could be done to a relationship that is important to you.

For example, during an election, politics is headline news. There are choices in your conversation. Asking if someone watched the debates or encouraging someone to express her opinions by voting is one thing. Urging someone to believe a certain way about a topic such as abortion or the death penalty is tempting an argument.

What do you really want to accomplish? If your goal is to get someone to think the way you do, that's fine. Engage in a conversation. If this is a business exchange, shift away from these topics:

- Politics
- Gender/sex
- Religion
- Weight
- Age
- Others at work
- Inappropriate jokes that could be offensive
- Getting too personal or sharing lots of personal information about yourself. (See the earlier comments about listening in the section "Listening Skills" later in the chapter.)

HOW TO REDIRECT A CONVERSATION

The real art of conversation is not only to say the right thing in the right place, but to leave unsaid the wrong thing at the tempting moment.

~ DOROTHY NEVILL

On occasion, we are in a conversation, and we realize that it is en route to becoming a runaway train. We sit there feeling a bit helpless as the conversation picks up speed and we begin to feel our uneasiness increasing. Think and think carefully! If the rapport between the two of you can withstand some friction, continue. If not, move the conversation to something that is more neutral and comfortable for you.

I was a dinner guest, and at one point the host asked a few questions about politics. I answered them politely, and then realized that he wanted to debate rather than to hear my point of view. The topic was a delicate one, and I could see that this was only going to get worse. At one point, I glanced over at the other side of the room and asked a question about the painting on the wall. I kept discussing the art in the home, and the discussion never returned to the delicate subject. When a conversation begins to go astray, take charge of your share. Decline to talk about anything you don't want to, and offer a new topic.

Be mindful that some people may have a less-than-honorable reason to ask questions. Think before you answer. You don't want to inappropriately (even if innocently) share information that isn't theirs to know.

HOW TO EXIT FROM A CONVERSATION

I've always been interested in people, but I've never liked them.

~ W. SOMERSET MAUGHAM

One of the questions I am asked most frequently is how to move away from someone without being rude. The conversation has reached its peak. There isn't much more to discuss. This happens on occasion when you meet someone who sells a product or service that you are not interested in. Do this person a favor and let him go talk to someone else. You are both nice people, but this is a business opportunity, and you both need to move onto other conversations.

Truthfully, the other person would probably like to move on as well, but he is just as nervous as you are. He has established a comfortable level with you. Starting a new conversation is work, so why bother? Why change a good thing?

Here are some pointers:

- Simply smile and say, "It was a pleasure meeting and/ or talking to you; enjoy your morning, evening, or the presentation."

- Include someone nearby in your conversation. When the two of them begin to converse, excuse yourself and get involved in a new conversation.

- Invite the person to join you as you walk over to the bar or food table. Typically you will meet at least one or two people on the way that you can include in your conversation.

- Never leave someone alone.

- Lying will make you feel dishonest because at that moment you are. Don't do it. Typical lies:

  - "I'm off to the restroom."
  - "I'm going to refresh my drink."

- In some situations, the conversation may be interesting and may merit another meeting. This frequently happens in a social situation where it just isn't appropriate to continue talking business and where you are likely to get interrupted at some point. Take charge! Don't risk being interrupted. Say to the other person that you'd like to follow up, ask for her card, shake hands, and move on. (See the section "Business Cards," in Chapter 5, for guidelines on when to hand them out.)

- When you are involved in an organization and you have a role, you also have permission to say to someone, "It's been nice talking to you. I need to say hello to others in the room, since I'm head of membership, and that's my job here."

LISTENING SKILLS

Be a good listener. Your ears will never get you in trouble.
~ FRANK TYGER

Every moment that people are talking, they are giving you an opportunity to offer help. Think about who in your network can help them. Make the introduction and make everyone happy.

When you listen, you can solve problems for others. This doesn't mean that you need to do all the work. Just recommend someone in your network who can help.

Here are some recommendations to help you improve your listening skills:

- *Stand up.* This works very well for people who are distracted when they are talking on the phone.
- *Don't do anything else.* Imagine that the person is right in front of you and deserves your total attention.
- *Face the person.* When you are standing a bit at an angle, it sends the message that you want to be open to leaving the conversation and are less interested.
- *Make eye contact.* Be aware of connecting to the other person every so often. Look at the color of his eyes—it's a great way of making good eye contact.
- *Count to three before you speak.*
- *Most important, concentrate on the other person's agenda, not yours.*

When you are focused on the other person, you come across as more confident. If your call really isn't genuine or you just want to make the connection to advance yourself, the other person can sense it quickly.

I was introduced to someone who was in charge of putting together events for an alumni association. We talked about dates for a presentation, what the group was looking for, who would be in the audience, and the typical questions I ask before a presentation. However, he quickly volunteered that he was unemployed and that this would be a good project for him to work on. He then shared with me the details about what he was looking for, how much networking he had done, and all the barriers that made it difficult for him to get a job.

He was a genuine person, and he certainly didn't realize that his actions were completely making me want to get off the phone and stay away! He talked too much and gave me too much information, and while he seemed eager to learn, his tactics indicated that he actually was not interested in improving his skills.

You may legitimately not know that you are doing something that is disruptive to someone else. I had a former boyfriend who used to finish my sentences. I finally said something to him about it. He then interrupted me and finished my sentence by asking what was my point.

We all have quirks. Find someone who is willing to tell you which of yours are charming and which are best unlearned. Talking too much can destroy a conversation very fast and is not uncommon. It usually happens when we are nervous. Be good to yourself and learn what are your strengths and what are your opportunities.

Summary: Knowing yourself can catapult you to networking success.

HOW LONG TO TALK TO SOMEONE

Some people can stay longer in an hour than others can in a week.

~ William Dean Howells

We all want to be remembered, but not as the person from whom someone could not get away. This is not the moment to share the philosophy behind your new business idea and why it is better than anything in existence. This is the moment to build rapport. This gives you the opportunity to follow up, ask for an appointment, and have a civilized meeting without interruptions.

An encounter at an event is a casual encounter. Networking is not a meeting, a sales call, or a job interview. One thing I can almost promise you: the conversation will be interrupted at least once, if not many times.

Your goal is to connect with the individual sufficiently that you can comfortably follow up and have her take your call.

Here are some thoughts to guide you:

- Talk for three to five minutes—a maximum of eight.
- If others are standing nearby, bring them into your conversation.
- Leave before you are left.
- If you want to follow up, say so and ask for a card.
- Be sure to follow up!

DON'T OVERSHARE

Sometimes when we meet people, we feel that we have found a long-lost friend. It is so refreshing to connect with someone who understands us and feels our joy (or pain). We laugh together, and we find that the conversation seems too short. Once I met someone socially who said that maybe she should come and get some networking help. By the end of the next drink, I knew about her divorce and her ex-in-laws, the fact that she had been fired from her last job, and her dislike of eating. She shared more information than I could possibly digest, and we had just met. Let your network nurture slowly. You are in there for the long haul.

Summary: Networking is like a fine meal. Slow down and savor the flavors and the experience.

8

Places to Network

NETWORKING WITHIN YOUR ORGANIZATION

An often-overlooked place to network is within your company or organization. Too often people put the emphasis on networking for clients, funding, or people. Without strong connections where you work, it is going to be difficult to succeed. Can you imagine if you need help on a project and you walk down the hall, introduce yourself, and ask the person to drop what they are doing and help you? Not likely.

One client was helping internal candidates get promoted. There was some friction because the men were getting promoted more often than the women. After some discussions and research about where the men were finding out about internal opportunities it turned out that most were over a casual conversation outside of the office.

Here's a suggestion—at least once a week invite someone to have a cup of coffee with you. Ask for 15-20 minutes and explain you've seen them at work but never really had a non-work conversation.

Some of the strongest friendships at work are created because people met in the Toastmasters Club or Weight Watchers group.

I often hear that people don't have time. I appreciate the situation. That's why I suggest you start with 15 minutes a week. After a month, ask yourself, did that 60 minutes of time invested in making a connection mean you were now better able to do your job? Or that you knew now who to go ask for help?

Summary: While you see colleagues frequently we often don't really know each other. Take time to build your internal network.

NETWORKING ON PLANES AND TRAINS

When you are in transit is an optimal time to practice your networking skills. First of all, the person you are talking to doesn't know you yet, so she has no preconceived notions of who you are and how you should behave. Second, you are in public, so if something goes awry, you can get away quickly. Third, something wonderful might happen. Here are some guidelines to help you maximize these situations:

- Carry a book and have it visible. When you first talk to someone, this indicates that you have something else to do and won't necessarily talk his ear off. Also, if the person turns out to be boring, you can begin reading right away.
- When you sit down, smile and say hello.
- Ask if she is heading to a meeting or heading home.
- Respect the person's personal space.
- Watch the person's body language—if the person shifts away from you, it's a sign that he wants to be left alone.
- On occasions I take a small knitting project with me. I'm not very good but I like lovely yarns and it's easy to knit and talk. Mind you once someone asked me if I was making

a gift for my grandchild. I gasped—didn't think I looked THAT old! What was she thinking? I even had weapon!

Summary: Informal networking opportunities are everywhere.

NETWORKING AT CONFERENCES AND TRADE SHOWS

At a trade show, people make up their mind in four seconds whether they will stop at your booth or not.[1] It is always crucial to make a strong first impression, and the stakes are higher at large events such as conferences and trade shows. Everyone on the team must reflect the image and style of the company at all times and in all places. That includes elevators, restaurants, planes, shuttle buses, and hotel lobbies, to name just a few.

Research Online before *the Conference*

Most people wait until they arrive at a conference, see the person they want to meet, and try to "catch" her while they are walking around. One person even got up early and went to the pool on the off chance of running into a journalist. *No!*

Use the Web to research people and contact them *before* you get there. It can be a simple e-mail, a phone call, or something in the mail.

Check the agenda and read the speaker's biography. A gutsy but high-impact technique is to e-mail the speaker ahead of time and ask if there is a question that he would like to have asked during the Q&A. That moment of silence between the applause following a speech and the Q&A can be painful for everyone if there aren't any questions. Get the questions started (and get a visible moment in front of the entire room) by raising your hand and asking the first one.

Take a look at the speaker's LinkedIn profile, Jigsaw, Facebook, or other online search tools. It used to be creepy to check people out, but this is now considered a basic business practice.

Book Appointments Ahead of Time

In many cases, you are attending a conference because there is someone specific that you want to meet with. Make the connection a week or so in advance. Explain why you'd like some time together. Be sure to state what problem you can solve. Don't overcommit yourself. You can quickly run out of time, and canceling appointments at shows is not professional.

I was attending a conference, so I read the bios of the speakers a few weeks ahead of time. It turned out that I had an alumni connection with one of them. Even though we hadn't met before, I sent a note mentioning the connection and saying that I'd be at the conference. We e-mailed a few times and then spoke. It turned out that she was looking for a consultant to help on a project. Next thing I knew, I had a paid project that I wouldn't have gotten if I hadn't contacted the speaker beforehand.

Working the Booth

Make a point of catching people's eye when they approach. Smile and say hello. If the person is also an exhibitor, ask a question such as how many shows he typically attends in a year or what in particular he likes about this one. If the person is an attendee, ask questions about her before you do too much talking. Then you will be able to tailor your comments to the individual.

Even if you aren't an extrovert you can do very well working at a booth. After all people are walking by you. Think friendly instead of extrovert! What would you want, to walk by and have someone barely notice you, or just say hello! Midwesterners are especially good at understanding the difference between extrovert and friendly. Often I am mistaken for an extrovert. Au contraire! But I am very friendly.

So Many Booths, So Little Time!

A show or conference can get overwhelming fast. The challenge is to identify in advance whom you want to see and why. Walk with someone else in the industry who is well known and respected. (Be sure you are not stalking that person—see the section "The Difference between Persistence and Stalking," in Chapter 11.)

Conferences can quickly become exhausting. While it's great to be away from the office, rarely does the mind truly shut down. Find a quiet place somewhere—in the convention hall, back at your room, in a restaurant—to gather your thoughts and be alone.

Remember, it's high-quality contacts that you are after. The number of business cards you get is not an indicator of future business. It's the quality of your interaction with the person who gave you the card that matters.

Get off the show floor. A lot of bonding happens off site. If you are invited to sponsored parties, be sure to attend, say hello to the person who invited you, and thank her as you leave.

Table for 20

When you attend a conference or a trade show, ask the concierge to book a dinner reservation for 20 at a nearby restaurant for the second evening of the conference. While you are meeting people at the conference, invite them to dinner. This is a great way to introduce people to one another, and you are the one who made it happen.

Before your boss hyperventilates at the idea of signing off on that expense account, this doesn't mean that you need to pick up the tab. You can organize something without paying for it. In fact, mention the name of the restaurant when you invite people and mention the price of a typical entrée. This signals that they are invited to attend, but that they are expected to pay their share.

Note: Let the server know in advance that everyone will want some type of individual receipt, and leave a very generous tip.

Summary: You help everyone avoid the problem of figuring out what to do for dinner in a strange town, you (and your company) gain visibility, and you connect strangers who are at the same conference for similar purposes.

NETWORKING AT JOB FAIRS

This is an excellent opportunity for you to have your ear to the ground and learn about various companies for which you would like to work. You can have conversations with other attendees and with companies that are interviewing. You can quickly get a sense of whether the company or the industry is one that you want to be a part of. Consider this to be valuable research time. Here are some thoughts on how to maximize the job fair experience:

- Dress for the job you want, not the one you have.
- Wear what you would wear if it were an interview—professional attire such as a suit or a jacket and tie.
- Look at your feet; do your shoes signal success?
- You have only one chance to make a first impression.
- Information interviews are just as important as "real" ones.
- If you don't do well here, you won't be recommended to others.
- Be able to tell your story; quickly, and from the viewpoint of what you'll do for the company and why it should hire you.
- Study the company's Web site.
- Do prep work about those you will be meeting. Search on Twitter, Facebook, and LinkedIn to find out more about the people who will be there.
- Have a good handshake and good eye contact.
- Smile!

- Stand up straight.
- Have a pen and paper to take notes.
- Treat everyone with respect; don't make any assumptions. I heard the story of a college student who managed to secure an interview at a job fair. He asked a woman from the company for a cup of coffee. As he settled in, he then asked one of the men when the vice president of sales was going to join them. The woman looked at him and said that she was the vice president of sales.
- Have a breath mint 15 minutes beforehand.
- Write an e-mail immediately to thank people for their time and ideas. Have a compelling subject line to differentiate you from the other candidates. I encourage you to write a handwritten thank-you note as well. The e-mail signals that you are efficient; the handwritten note says that you are a mature, polite, and professional person.
- Strike up a conversation with the organizers of the job fair. They know the inside scoop!
- Talk to other candidates in line. Just because you are all job hunters does not mean that you are all competing for the same job.

Summary: Job fairs are a great place to practice and tone your skills.

NETWORKING AT MEETINGS

Before you attend the meeting, ask for a list of attendees. Research them online so that you have starter conversations. In my bio, I note that I took stand-up comedy classes in order to get over my fear of public speaking. I also say that I "attempt" to play tennis. It's fun when someone has taken the time to read my bio. It sends a signal to me that this person is focused on the meeting and is prepared.

The first few minutes of a meeting are an excellent time to network. The atmosphere is casual, and the conversation is light. Take advantage of the mood and get to know others in the room. While this is written from the perspective of a meeting with outsiders present, the principles can be applied to internal meetings as well. Here are some thoughts:

- Determine who the note taker is. (When in doubt, you should take the notes.)
- Arrive as early as you can. This avoids the angst of walking into a room full of strangers.
- Stand up when you meet someone, shake hands, and maintain good eye contact. This is true for both men and women.
- Exchange business cards at the beginning of the meeting. Either place the cards in front of you in the order in which people sit around the table or draw a diagram of the meeting participants with their names. This will help you remember who people are.
- Ask two or three neutral questions. Some examples include
  ○ How did you all first meet?
  ○ Have you done business together before?
  ○ Where did you work before?
- When taking notes, date the first page and number all pages.
- Have clear "next step" actions written out.
- At the end, go around, thank others for attending, and shake hands.
- If there are people from out of town, make sure that they have directions to their next destination.

Summary: We often assume if we are in an internal meeting that it doesn't present a networking opportunity. Nothing could be further from the truth. Value this time. Learn how to run a meeting and you will get noticed.

Why I Started Boston Media Makers

Steve Garfield, founder of Boston Media Makers

Steve Garfield started Boston Media Makers after finding that he was frustrated at not being able to meet every single person in the room at a local conference. Someone stood up to ask a question, and he seemed very interesting. That's when Steve thought, "There are 295 other really interesting people in this room, and I am never going to be able to meet them!" So he started Boston Media Makers so that everyone who attends will be able to hear from everyone else in the room. I asked him to share the story of how the group came to be, once his initial idea was in place:

I contacted a few people and asked them to join me for a drink at a local bar. One person showed up. We had a great chat, and I took some photos. I made up a Web site, posted the photos, and wrote up a meeting report, then posted the date for the next meeting. That time a few more people came. Then I chose a regular date, time, and place to meet. After each meeting, I'd post meeting notes and photos to show what happened so that people who might be interested could see what it's like.

Today, Boston Media Makers get together at Doyle's in Jamaica Plain on the first Sunday of each month from 10 a.m. to noon. We gather around a big table and answer the question, "What are you doing?"

If you are interested in meeting people who are working with audio and video on the Web, this is a great meeting to attend. We get podcasters, videobloggers, filmmakers, artists, writers, and PR and social media people. Everyone is welcome.

Sometimes we have a roundtable discussion after we hear from everyone, but there usually isn't extra time. It's fun.

How to Run a Media Makers Meeting

Welcome: Explain how Media Makers started so that everyone will get a chance to hear from everyone else. Thank the venue, introduce the server, and explain that the check will go around at the end and everyone pays with a nice tip.

Tagging: Give the tag for any content that anyone makes on any medium, including blog posts, photos, and video, for example, #NYCMM011109. (Appending the tag to everything posted makes that content *searchable* on Flickr, Twitter, blogs, and other such sites.).

Tweets: Ask people to tweet meeting notes and links. There's no expectation of privacy; your photo, audio, and video will be taken. If you don't want to be photographed, let us know.

Agenda: To start, I do a roll call video and everyone says his name and his URL if he has one. Then we take a half hour to mingle, and get everyone chatting and exchanging contacts. No sitting! Over the next hour and a half, each person takes about 3 minutes to explain what she is doing, state what she is interested in, or ask a question. People should stand up when they talk. They also have the opportunity to do a simple show and tell. Some people bring cameras, accessories, all kinds of things. It's also a great idea to ask if anyone has any questions at the start (if folks can stay for only a limited time, for example). We prefer no sales presentations—it's not a pitch; it's networking! Toward the end, have the bill go around and people contribute.

Venue: Don't pay for a venue. Don't make people pay to attend.

Upcoming events: Post future meetings on upcoming.org so that prospective attendees can see who's registered to attend. A Facebook group is a good idea too.

Numbers: Boston Media Makers appears to have a good size—approximately 40 folks at the last meeting. This allows everyone to mingle and really get to know each other.

Timing: Have the meeting in the same place every month, and even the same location if you can arrange it.

Blog: After each meeting, you've got to make a blog post with photos from the meeting and some notes, so that people who missed the meeting can see what it's like. Videos are great too, especially short ones of interesting moments. Artistic videos too. We like to post photos that afternoon.

If users tag content with the same tag (in our case, #BMMMMDDYY —BMM: Boston Media Makers; MMDDYY: month, date, year), we can find them all on Flickr and in the social Web.

9

Best Practices

There is nothing that builds confidence more than knowing best practices. When you need to know them isn't the time to learn them. Start now! This has nothing to do with wealth or education; it has everything to do with self-respect.

Look carefully at this chapter, and keep practicing until you can properly teach someone else. Best practices make it easier to get things done in life. You can relax and stay focused on your conversation.

Knowing best practices gives us peace of mind, as we know how to conduct ourselves. Being familiar with the right thing to do in the right circumstances gives you confidence. Learn these practices and use them now! Eliminate anything that blocks you from furthering any business relationship you have or want to have.

MANNERS

> *Your manners are always under examination, and by committees little suspected, awarding or denying you very high prizes when you least think it.*
>
> ~ RALPH WALDO EMERSON

Manners are both the cake and the icing. Dessert just isn't quite right with only one or the other. You never hear people complain that someone's manners are too good. In fact, when manners are done right, they are invisible. That's the point: there is only an upside to knowing and practicing proper manners. For networking, here are a few highlights:

- *Handshakes.* Both men and women should shake hands. Ladies, some men have been raised to not extend their hand unless you do so first. Therefore, put your hand out and greet the other person.

- *Dining.* If you make the invitation, you select the restaurant. You also should plan to pay. Make advance arrangements with the wait staff to pay for the meal so that this is seamless. Even if the person you are with is on an expense account, you want to acknowledge that she is personally giving you her time.

- *Alcohol.* Don't drink during the day, and be cautious in the evening. Always give up your car keys if requested.

- *Smoking.* Just don't smoke.

- *Conversations.* Discuss, never debate.

- *Flirting.* This is business. Flirt at another time and place.

- *Jokes.* Don't tell any joke you wouldn't want your kids or your grandmother to hear (and repeat). This says something about your integrity, too.

- *Invitations.* Respond within five days of *receiving* an invitation.

- *Attire.* Ask the host what is appropriate, and comply.

- *Briefcase.* This wonderful container of your life sits on the subway floor and the trunk and floor of your car, not to mention restrooms and other places. Don't plop it on a lovely wood conference table or a chair.

- ***For gentlemen.*** Open doors and walk on the outside of the street. Few men do this anymore, and it will be noticed even if it isn't commented on.

Manners open doors that power, position, and money cannot. Learning the "rules" of business etiquette is easy; they are 80% common sense and 20% kindness.
     ~ DANA MAY CASPERSON, author of *Power Etiquette*

THE RECEPTIONIST OR EXECUTIVE ASSISTANT

There is a reason that the term *gatekeeper* is used. This person is a protector. If you have one, you know the value of this. If you are working with someone else's, he can be your facilitator to success—or your worst enemy. Get the gatekeeper to believe in what you want to accomplish. Be friendly, respectful, and courteous at all times.

If you have a receptionist or executive administrator, here are some reminders:

- Thank her frequently.
- Make sure that he knows your expectations on how to make people feel welcome.
- This person is your most important ambassador.
- Teach the person how to answer the phone and greet your guests. She is your client's first impression of you and your business. How she looks, talks, and behaves reflects on both you and the company.
- Invest in this person.
- Use the words *please* and *thank you* often when speaking with him.
- Have a clear policy about what topics are and are not appropriate for her to discuss with any visitors.

- Also do the same for Web surfing in a public setting.
- Have drinks or water nearby.

INTRODUCTIONS

This simple gesture sets the tone of a conversation. It often provides ways to start the conversation as well. How you introduce yourself and others will make them feel connected or rejected. Just as with manners, learn some quick ways to make introductions and feel confident doing so.

Introduce Yourself

It is crucial that you have an introduction that you like and can easily say. I've heard some that are quite complicated and overwhelming. Note that an introduction is different from your elevator pitch, which may or may not follow an introduction depending on the circumstances. The elevator pitch is typically around 30 seconds and sounds a bit like a sales pitch. These became quite popular during the "dot-com" days.

Your introduction should invite a conversation and be extremely brief—no more than 5 to 10 seconds at the most. If you want to learn a great way to introduce yourself, just listen to the parent of a little one. For many years my mother had no name . . . she was just "Diane's mom." In the business world, we typically say our name first, but by the time the person understands how we are connected to the situation, he can't remember our name.

I suggest that you switch it around—say your name *after* you say something about yourself.

Therefore, a good introduction should include three things:

1. How you fit into the situation
2. Your name
3. Why the other person should care

Use words such as *help, provide, contribute, give, serve, teach,* and *solve*. The introduction is about what you can do for others, not what they can do for you. Your introduction is successful if it invites questions. If it shuts down the conversation, it was unsuccessful, and you need to rework it.

Here are some examples:

- "I'm an exhibitor at this show from People Technology, my name is Susan Smith, and we help companies find the right people for their technology positions."
- "I'm a speaker at the conference, my name is George Adams, and I help companies identify and execute their marketing strategy."

Here is an example at a meeting:

- "I'm in the finance department, my name is John Dunn, and I'm here to help with the business plan."

This is awkward when you first try it. Just practice and it will become easier. I encourage you to say the phrase "my name is" because this phrase will slow you down and indicate to the listener: I'm going to hear a name.

You may want to add something humorous. During one of the training sessions for relationship managers at a bank, a gentleman said that he "managed relationships but couldn't help out with the one at home." It got a good laugh and was very memorable.

When men first meet, they immediately introduce themselves. Women sometimes do, but not as frequently.

Summary: In business, you should simply say who you are and what is your connection to the meeting, event, or whatever you may be attending. As much as possible, provide information that will spark a dialogue.

One Size Doesn't Fit All

You need to master a variety of introductions—after all, you have multiple roles. If you are at your child's baseball game, introducing yourself with your title from work would come across as odd, to say the least, as would the opposite—for example, if you were at a conference and you introduced yourself as Jimmy's dad.

Introduce Someone Else

When you are meeting business professionals, you are often called upon to introduce other people. This can be a formal introduction or something more casual. Use this opportunity as an excellent way to get conversations started. If the introductions are in a more formal setting, here are some guidelines to follow for the proper order:

- Younger to older
- Junior to senior
- Company employee to guest company individual
- Your executive to customer or client

Other pointers:

- Start with the person's name.
- Then give her title or role.
- Give the name of the company (if necessary).
- Mention something that is unique about the person.

Here's a sample introduction: "Susan Jones, I would like you to meet Jack Collins, our vice president of marketing. Jack, this is Susan, our new manager of customer service. Jack is an avid sailor. Susan sails at the MIT Yacht Club."

Names

Using someone's name is important when making introductions. Here are some guidelines.

- Learn what name the person actually uses. For example, is it Richard or Rick, Deborah or Deb?
- Use a nickname only if that is what the person uses in business.
- For unusual pronunciations, practice ahead of time, and don't hesitate to ask the person again. It's better than punting and getting it wrong.
- If someone walks up to you and you should introduce him, but you don't remember the names of the people you are with, introduce yourself and then invite the others to introduce themselves.
- See the section "How to Remember Names," in Chapter 10.

OVERNETWORKING

With so many networking opportunities available, choosing the ones that are best for us can seem daunting. The dilemma is worsened by the explosion of online and hybrid networking options. Given all this, it is easy to overnetwork, forcing ourselves to attend events. This leads to burnout and to wasted networking opportunities. Not a good idea!

Another form of overnetworking is being too aggressive with your contacts. Most of us are guilty of "dropping the ball" sometimes when it comes to following up with networking contacts. Don't assume that the opportunity is lost if you have not been conscientious about cultivating a given contact. On the other hand, don't make the mistake of jumping right back into a conversation as though months (or years!) had not passed since you last spoke. When the economy shifted recently, I started receiving calls from people I had met more than a year ago and had never heard from since, asking, "When can I take you to lunch?" My first thought was, who *are* you?

Both kinds of overnetworking are avoidable. They are most common when we are nervous and/or disorganized. This can easily be fixed with a few changes to your behavior. I offered tips for overscheduling in Chapter 8. You should also ask yourself the following questions from your contact "Whether Report." (See Figure 4-5 on page 81.)

For an event (online or in person), ask yourself:

- Is there someone whose opinion I respect and who has attended the event before who can advise me whether or not this is worth my time?
- Am I able to introduce myself confidently?
- Have I had a good day, or am I feeling grumpy?

For a face-to-face event, ask yourself:

- Have I had a bad hair day? (See the Yale study mentioned in Chapter 4, on page 67.)
- Do I have business cards with me?
- If I walk into the event and I don't get my energy in 10 minutes, will I give myself permission to leave without berating myself?

When contacting or speaking with individuals, ask yourself:

- When did I last communicate with this person?
- What were the circumstances?
- Will he know me by name?
- What is my ultimate goal in making this call? Do I want information, support, a job lead, an introduction, or something else?
- How will I determine if the interaction is a success?

For a phone call to a specific person, ask yourself:

- Am I making it easy for this person to help me?
- What am I asking of this person?
- Is it something that she can do?
- If she called in the past, did I take the call or return it promptly?
- Have I written out a list of the things I want to ask this person? Have I practiced out loud what I want to say?
- Have I received permission from the introducer to use his name?
- Am I ready to speak right now if this person can give me a few minutes immediately?
- If she wants to schedule an appointment, is my calendar open, and do I know my availability?
- If you want to schedule a meeting, suggest some dates and follow up.

For a meeting, ask yourself:

- Has this person given me advice before?
- If so, did I follow it? If not, why not? Will I be able to explain it?
- Do I have pen and paper ready to take notes?
- Is my cell phone *off*?

Overnetworking online is a bit tougher to self-monitor. I don't have any specific time guidelines. I will say that if you are networking only online, it's probably not as effective. Unless you are marooned on an island and online is all you have, I suggest that you follow the hybrid model that I've described, utilizing a variety of channels tailored to the individual you want to connect with and/or the goal you want to achieve. Social networking sites are a great research tool. They can also provide a way to initiate conversations with individuals that you want to contact or to build relationships you have started face-to-face. However, relying purely on online interaction usually will not serve to establish a robust network. A variety of offline events are promoted within the online social network communities. Take advantage of these (subject to the overscheduling guidelines described earlier) to get to know people that you may have interacted with only online. It is well worth the effort.

It's all about results. If you find you are accomplishing your networking goals mainly online, that's fine. Just don't get too isolated. The first language this book was translated into was Korean. I was surprised, and McGraw-Hill explained that Korea has a highly educated population that is young, its Internet is much faster than that in the United States, and Koreans tend to do almost everything online. Therefore, books about people skills do quite well at encouraging people to balance their online and offline lives.

Summary: Invest some time in your preparation. You will show up at events that are interesting and worth your while. When you do that, you are typically a happier and more likable person. That will attract people to you and your business. When you are networking online, follow the same guidelines as you would in person. It's all on record—would you really want to see it in the headlines?

Fashion Fit Formula

Janet Wood, the CEO of the Fashion Fit Formula

She has been in business for 35 years and owes much of her success to networking. When I asked her to detail her thoughts on networking, this is what she told me:

What I have found is that you must be willing to give freely, be humorous, and follow up. After meeting new contacts, I always take a moment to write a personal note on their business card. That night, without fail, I enter it into my computer contact database. I always send a follow-up e-mail stating that I enjoyed meeting this person, that I have an extensive network, and that if the person needs something in regard to his career (customers, a new job, and so on), to drop me an e-mail and I will do what I can to help him. It has been very effective, and I have been able to put many people together and make deals happen. They always remember me, and they are always willing to help me in return.

I am fairly new to online networking. However, by going through my database, I have been able to reconnect online with people who over time had fallen off the radar screen. Through one of these contacts, I agreed to interview a third party for a very high paying position. Her résumé was impressive—we chatted via Twitter, and it all looked very promising.

I was running late arriving at my office for the interview, and I caught the elevator at the last minute. Between the third and the fourth floors, the elevator stopped. We were told via the emergency equipment that it would take about 20 minutes for them to get it fixed. The elevator was crowded, and one young woman was quite rude. She chewed gum with her mouth open and made disparaging comments about being late for her interview.

I mentioned that I was sure whoever was interviewing her would be understanding. She replied that she had the job in the bag, but she wanted to get the interview over with fast so that she could get to a certain bar in hopes of reconnecting with a man she had met the night before. I asked her if the job wasn't more important. Laughing, she said that it was more important to her parents that she get a prestigious job, since they had paid for her four-year party at Princeton University!

Needless to say, you know who turned out to be the candidate for the position. Once the elevator started to work, we both got off and headed to the same door. I then asked her name; upon hearing it, I smiled, put out my hand, and told her that the "interview" had provided all the information I needed for a decision.

Moral of the story, you are always on "show," and some of the best business connections can be made in an elevator.

10

Best Practices when You Are
Face-to-Face

From the time you walk in the door until the time you walk out, this
chapter will provide a step-by-step guide to successfully navigat-
ing a networking event. Take a look at the "XPlanation" diagram in
Figure 10-1. This gives you a visual step-by-step guide.

Wear something that makes you feel confident and will make
it easier for someone to describe you. Men can wear a tie with a nice
design, and women can wear a suit in a color other than navy, brown,
or black.

Before you head to an event, conference, or meeting, you need to
pack your Networking Survival Kit. The purpose is to have everything
you need for networking in one place. When you head out the door, you
can grab the kit and everything is stocked and ready to go.

PACKING LIST FOR YOUR NETWORKING SURVIVAL KIT

The idea behind packing your Networking Survival Kit[1] is to ensure
that you have everything you need or want readily at hand. There

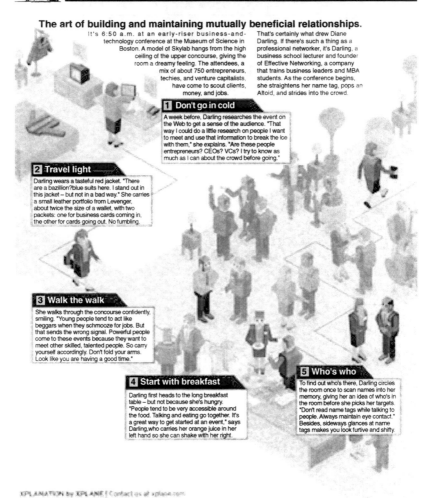

The art of building and maintaining mutually beneficial relationships.

It's 6:50 a.m. at an early-riser business-and-technology conference at the Museum of Science in Boston. A model of Skylab hangs from the high ceiling of the upper concourse, giving the room a dreamy feeling. The attendees, a mix of about 750 entrepreneurs, techies, and venture capitalists, have come to scout clients, money, and jobs.

That's certainly what drew Diane Darling. If there's such a thing as a professional networker, it's Darling, a business school lecturer and founder of Effective Networking, a company that trains business leaders and MBA students. As the conference begins, she straightens her name tag, pops an Altoid, and strides into the crowd.

1 Don't go in cold

A week before, Darling researches the event on the Web to get a sense of the audience. "That way I could do a little research on people I want to meet and use that information to break the ice with them," she explains. "Are these people entrepreneurs? CEOs? VCs? I try to know as much as I can about the crowd before going."

2 Travel light

Darling wears a tasteful red jacket. "There are a bazillion?blue suits here. I stand out in this jacket – but not in a bad way." She carries a small leather portfolio from Levenger, about twice the size of a wallet, with two packets: one for business cards coming in, the other for cards going out. No fumbling.

3 Walk the walk

She walks through the concourse confidently, smiling. "Young people tend to act like beggars when they schmooze for jobs. But that sends the wrong signal. Powerful people come to these events because they want to meet other skilled, talented people. So carry yourself accordingly. Don't fold your arms. Look like you are having a good time."

4 Start with breakfast

Darling first heads to the long breakfast table – but not because she's hungry. "People tend to be very accessible around the food. Talking and eating go together. It's a great way to get started at an event," says Darling,who carries her orange juice in her left hand so she can shake with her right.

5 Who's who

To find out who's there, Darling circles the room once to scan names into her memory, giving her an idea of who's in the room before she picks her targets. "Don't read name tags while talking to people. Always maintain eye contact." Besides, sideways glances at name tags makes you look furtive and shifty.

XPLANATION by XPLANE | Contact us at xplane.com

Figure 10-1 XPLANATION

Source: XPLANE (xplane.com). First appeared in *MBA Jungle Magazine*, March/April 2002. (http://effectivenetworking.com/content/effectivenetworking/)

is nothing worse than realizing that you've left your business cards behind or you don't have a pen. As discussed in the previous chapter "Best Practices," make it easy and less stressful on yourself. Have this kit ready to go. You may wish to pack several—one for your briefcase, another for the car, and one for your office. If there is some wonderful product or tool that we missed, send an e-mail to KIT@ EffectiveNetworking.com.

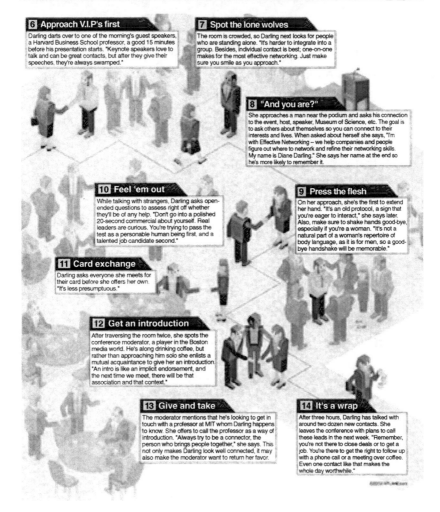

6 Approach V.I.P's first

Darling darts over to one of the morning's guest speakers, a Harvard Business School professor, a good 15 minutes before his presentation starts. "Keynote speakers love to talk and can be great contacts, but after they give their speeches, they're always swamped."

7 Spot the lone wolves

The room is crowded, so Darling next looks for people who are standing alone. "It's harder to integrate into a group. Besides, individual contact is best; one-on-one makes for the most effective networking. Just make sure you smile as you approach."

8 "And you are?"

She approaches a man near the podium and asks his connection to the event, host, speaker, Museum of Science, etc. The goal is to ask others about themselves so you can connect to their interests and lives. When asked about herself she says, "I'm with Effective Networking – we help companies and people figure out where to network and refine their networking skills. My name is Diane Darling." She says her name at the end so he's more likely to remember it.

10 Feel 'em out

While talking with strangers, Darling asks open-ended questions to assess right off whether they'll be of any help. "Don't go into a polished 20-second commercial about yourself. Real leaders are curious. You're trying to pass the test as a personable human being first, and a talented job candidate second."

9 Press the flesh

On her approach, she's the first to extend her hand. "It's an old protocol, a sign that you're eager to interact," she says later. Also, make sure to shake hands good-bye, especially if you're a woman. "It's not a natural part of a woman's repertoire of body language, as it is for men, so a good-bye handshake will be memorable."

11 Card exchange

Darling asks everyone she meets for their card before she offers her own. "It's less presumptuous."

12 Get an introduction

After traversing the room twice, she spots the conference moderator, a player in the Boston media world. He's alone drinking coffee, but rather than approaching him solo she enlists a mutual acquaintance to give her an introduction. "An intro is like an implicit endorsement, and the next time we meet, there will be that association and that context."

13 Give and take

The moderator mentions that he's looking to get in touch with a professor at MIT whom Darling happens to know. She offers to call the professor as a way of introduction. "Always try to be a connector, the person who brings people together," she says. This not only makes Darling look well connected, it may also make the moderator want to return her favor.

14 It's a wrap

After three hours, Darling has talked with around two dozen new contacts. She leaves the conference with plans to call these leads in the next week. "Remember, you're not there to close deals or to get a job. You're there to get the right to follow up with a phone call or a meeting over coffee. Even one contact like that makes the whole day worthwhile."

Kit for an Event, Conference, Trade Show, or Meeting

- Your business cards.
- Two business card cases, one for your cards and the other for the cards you receive. I suggest that both be memorable; they can perhaps inspire a conversation.
- Pen, either one that is memorable or one that you can lose.

- Note cards—start with 3″ × 5″ cards or a small notebook.
- Sharpie marker—for your name badge.
- Breath mints—a must!
- Directions to the event.
- Printout of the front page of the hosting organization's Web site.
- Printout of the staff and board members for the organization.
- For a meeting, add
  - ○ Portfolio for taking notes.
  - ○ Copies of the personal snapshots of everyone who will be at the meeting.

If you arrive without something that you need, you will come across as apathetic and uninterested. It's amazing how many people show up for meetings without a pen and paper. Curiously, it's often the CEOs who have both and the junior people who don't. *Think like a CEO!* Be ready to accept help and share information.

While your business cards and other networking tools are important, so are the intangible networking tools. Be sure to pack these as well:

- Smile
- Tall posture
- Positive attitude
- Curiosity
- Sense of humor

Networking Survival Kit for the Office

There is nothing worse than getting ready to head to an event or a meeting and realizing that you have dog hair on your suit coat or that your hem has come out. Put together a small kit for your drawer at work and/or your car.

- Toothbrush and paste
- Hand lotion
- Nail file, clippers, and/or polish
- Comb and/or brush
- Hair spray
- Lint brush
- Cosmetics/shaving kit
- Tissues
- Socks/hosiery
- Moist towelettes
- Breath mints
- Safety pins
- Sewing kit

NAME BADGES OR NAVEL DECORATIONS?

I'm not talking about military brass; I'm talking about your belly button. While the badge holders with long straps have their advantages (e.g., they don't puncture your clothes), it is extremely uncomfortable talking to someone whose eyes keep dropping to read the name tag in that *personal* territory.

Women who place their name badge south of their shoulder and north of their waist are asking for attention to an area that they otherwise would not want people to focus on. Here are some basics:

- Name badges aren't for you; they are for the other person.
- Carry a Sharpie marker.
- When you arrive at an event, print your name in large letters instead of using the ballpoint pen at the registration

desk. The person who may give you business or a job just might be over 40.

- If you're gutsy, add something memorable. For example, suppose you are a relationship manager at a bank. Here's your name tag: "Dan, the Dr. Phil of Business Banking." It's guaranteed to start a conversation.

- Name badges go on your right shoulder. (Left is for the Pledge of Allegiance.) Why the right side? When you shake hands, the eye naturally travels up the right arm. Make it easy for the person and don't force him to do a "chest scan" to read your name. Put your name badge high on your shoulder so that people can look in your eyes when they greet you.

Summary: Your name badge is a tool to allow others to learn and remember your name. Make it easy (and professional) for them to do so.

HANDSHAKE

Your handshake communicates a powerful nonverbal message before you speak. A firm handshake conveys confidence, assurance, interest and respect. A limp handshake can send the opposite message.

~ DANA MAY CASPERSON

Have you ever received a bad handshake? Ah! There is the vice grip handshake, and then there are the people who prefer to slap a dead fish in your palm.

You want people to remember *you*, not your handshake. Your handshake is one of the most important communication tools you have. Use it to your advantage. You want to communicate that you are friendly, you can get things done, and you know how to conduct yourself in a business situation. You do not want to communicate that you are aloof, uncertain of your abilities, unprofessional, or on a power trip.

I was working with a female senior executive who was looking for a job. At the end of our first session, I went to shake her hand and say good-bye. Her handshake was terrible! Here she was seeking an executive-level role, and her handshake felt as if she was in elementary school. I asked her to shut the door. She knew immediately. She said, "I have a bad handshake, don't I?"

We practiced handshakes a few times, and when I met her the next time, she was all smiles. She told me that she went home that night and told her husband that she had a bad handshake. He commented that he wasn't sure they had ever shaken hands. What a surprise! Most husbands and wives don't shake hands, and that's just fine. He agreed that her handshake wasn't good. Over the next week, she practiced as much as she possibly could and gained confidence in the process.

Good handshakes are easy to learn. What's important is that you have someone who is honest with you. Typically I wear a ring on my right hand. If there is a dent in my skin in the shape of the ring I'm wearing, then the handshake is too strong. When I show the person the physical remnant of his handshake, he is really surprised and appreciative that someone has told him.

No one wants to offend another person. However, letting someone repeat behavior that diminishes her chance of success isn't helping that person, it's hurting her. The key is to communicate your message carefully.

Use this book as an excuse to tell someone about the importance of handshakes. Ask this person to test yours. What does the person like about it? What doesn't feel right? Do this with people of both genders. Also test your handshake with people who are in their sixties or older. You don't want to crush anyone's fragile bones.

"Handshaking, Gender, Personality, and First Impressions"[2] is a formal study that was conducted at the University of Alabama

Department of Psychology. It was written up in the July 2000 issue of the *Journal of Personality and Social Psychology.*

It states that "a firm handshake was related positively to extra-version and emotional expressiveness and negatively to shyness and neuroticism." In some cases, it isn't until after the handshake and introduction that we have had a chance to say a single word to the other person. The smile may be welcoming, and then, yuck—a dead fish handshake. Let several people in your business network know that you are reading this book and ask them to critique your handshake.

History of the Handshake

The handshake started in medieval times when people who met would look at the other's right hand to see if there was a weapon in it. To signify trust, they would stretch out their right hand, indicating that it was safe to approach.

Characteristics of a Handshake

Today, in most cases, shaking hands isn't life-threatening. However, there are many people out there who were never taught a proper handshake. The University of Alabama study concluded that there was indeed a relationship between the characteristics of a handshake (strength, vigor, completeness of grip, duration, and eye contact) and a positive first impression.

Note: This information is applicable for doing business in the United States. In other countries and cultures, however, there are other greetings that are appropriate. It is recommended that you research the local customs prior to traveling.

A handshake is straightforward. Here's how it works:

- Look at your right hand. Notice the skin between your thumb and your index finger. It's soft and webby, just like a duck's webbed foot. This part of your hand should touch the other person's right hand. Think, web touching web or thumb aiming at thumb.

- Next, the palms of the hands should touch lightly. You don't want to cup your hand. This makes people wonder what you are hiding inside it.

- Finally, shake up and down slightly or hold for a moment and then . . . *let go*! It's amazing how many people forget that part.

- Maintain eye contact throughout the handshake and the introduction.

- After the handshake, ask yourself, do I remember the color of the person's eyes? This is a good test of whether or not you have paid attention during the introduction.

- A reminder to ladies, extend your hand. In business, it's a signal of confidence and equality.

Handshakes to Avoid

Here are some frequently used, and sometimes misused, handshakes.

- ***Bill Clinton handshake.*** Many people have the image of our fine former president shaking hands with his right hand while placing his left hand on the person's shoulder. This should be done only if the two parties know each other quite well. Men should use caution if they do it to women, especially women they don't know. In other words, ask your attorney first. Touching above the elbow can be grounds for a sexual harassment claim.

- ***Churchlady handshake.*** This is when someone puts his left hand on top of the two right ones that are shaking, as if to say, "Aren't you cute, dear, so nice to see you." Handshakes are between two hands, not three.

- *"I'm in charge" handshake.* These people aren't quite sure that they actually are in charge, so just to make sure, while shaking hands, they rotate their hand ever so slightly so that theirs is on top. This subtle message says, "I'm superior."
- *"What year did you graduate?" handshake.* This is for the people who lost an arm-wrestling contest at summer camp and have been trying to recover ever since. While shaking your hand, he grips so tightly that his graduation year, so delicately engraved on his class ring, is now permanently embedded in the side of your finger. Most likely he means no harm, and he also has no clue as to how strong he is.

Men Shake and Women Kiss—What to Do?

During a recent discussion on this topic, an accomplished professional mentioned that he was teaching his 8-year-old son to shake hands, but he wasn't teaching his 10-year-old daughter.

Men shake hands all the time. Just watch them. They say hello with a handshake, and they also say good-bye with one. They say congratulations with a handshake. This is true in both social settings and professional ones.

Women have not been raised to shake hands when they see each other in business or social settings. Men who have been brought up with traditional manners have been told not to put their hand out until the woman does. In a business setting, gender should not matter— everyone should shake hands with everyone else.

> *Summary: A firm handshake signals confidence and the ability to get things done.*

HOW TO REMEMBER NAMES

My memory is so bad that many times I forget my own name.

~ DON QUIXOTE

You've just met someone, and less than a second later you have no idea what the person's name is. This is often one of the most embarrassing and awkward moments in networking. With a few techniques, you can reverse this painful instant and come across as polished and professional. A person's name is melodic to her ears; use it. I have yet to meet a single person who has not had her name misspelled or even been called by the wrong name altogether. It happens no matter how simple or how complex the name is.

Ask yourself, would I pay more attention to someone's name if I knew that when I walked out of here, I would get a new client, a donation for my nonprofit, or a new job?

Here are some helpful ways to remember names:

- *Think of $100 per name.* Remember Benjamin Franklin and the "club for mutual improvement"? His face graces the $100 bill. If I promised to give you a $100 bill for each name that you remembered, would you try harder? My guess is that you would indeed get a number of names right. Whatever motivates you to learn names, do it! Really try!

- *Get it right the first time.* When someone introduces himself and you haven't heard the name or can't say it, simply ask the person to repeat it.

- *Spell it back.* This shows that you are genuinely interested in getting it right.

- *Use the name.* In the first few sentences, use the person's name once or twice. Don't do it too often, or it will appear pretentious and can quickly become annoying.

- *Ask a question.* If you know someone else with the same name, ask if there is a relation. Or ask what the derivation of the name is. We have become so politically correct that we don't want to offend anyone; on the other hand, we are willing to walk around mispronouncing someone's name (assuming that we heard it to begin with).

- **Connect the name to something.** If you know someone with the same name, make a mental note of the connection. For example, I used to work with someone named Susan Fleming—just like Ian Fleming, who wrote the James Bond books. Remember whom the person is with when you meet and make the connection to that person.

- **Be cautious about your word association.** When I was teaching, someone shared this story with me. There was someone named Chip, and he couldn't remember the nickname, especially since it was for a woman. So he thought of his favorite chip—a chocolate chip cookie. The next time he saw her, he smiled and said, "Hi, Cookie!"

- **Write the name down.** When you are in a meeting and people are introducing themselves, pull out a piece of paper and write each person's name with a few words.

- **Use tent cards.** If you are hosting a meeting, provide tent cards. Bring an 8½″ × 11″ piece of paper, fold it lengthwise, and use it as a tent card. Construction paper works just fine.

- **Create a system that works for you.** If you remember things visually, mentally write the person's name down. If you are an auditory person, say it out loud. If you are a kinesthetic learner, write it with your toe in the carpet or image it in the sky.

- **Make it easy for others.** If for whatever reason—logical or not—others don't get your name right, take responsibility, and when you introduce yourself, make it easy. Typically I say, "I'm Diane Darling—just like sweetheart." If someone is writing it down, I'll add, "That's Diane with one *n*." Other people are not intentionally trying to clobber your

name. However, they may be nervous, confused, tired—
who knows. Make them feel better by helping them out.

*Summary: Saying someone's name gets that person's
attention. When you have someone's attention, you can
build rapport and make a personal connection.*

FOOD AND BEVERAGES

This is network, not net-eat!

~ AUTHOR

Most networking events involve eating in some fashion, whether it's
a breakfast meeting, a cocktail party, or a sit-down dinner. We can
quickly become distracted by the food and forget why we are attending in the first place. If you have to eat as a part of the event, then do
so. Otherwise, consider having a snack before you head out so that
you can focus on your conversation, and not your stomach.

Pick Your Priorities—Muffin or Money

Early one morning, I drove to Cape Cod to attend a forum for entrepreneurs and investors. I'm not particularly a morning person, but I
had a business idea that I wanted to get funded. This was just such
an opportunity.

As I scrambled to get out the door, I decided to forgo breakfast,
since there would certainly be food at the event. I drove for 90 minutes and arrived shortly after 7 a.m. By this time my brain was wide
awake, and so was my stomach.

I checked in and headed to grab a glass of juice and a muffin. At
that very moment, a conversation began about my brilliant business
idea and what capital would be required to get it off the ground. The
dialogue was very engaging, and this individual, himself an investor, wanted to make some introductions on my behalf. We walked a
few steps as I attempted to juggle the juice glass and muffin as well

as a briefcase. As I put my hand out to greet the person I was being introduced to, the muffin lost.

I stood there as animated as Mount Rushmore as I watched the muffin roll down the hall. What I had forgotten that morning was to select a priority. Was it food, or was it appearing professional in front of an investor? The entire situation could have been avoided if I had gotten up a few minutes earlier and had a bite at home or taken a nutrition bar with me and eaten in the car.

Munch with Your Networking Buddy

If I arrive hungry, I find someone I know well, preferably someone whom I see frequently in business or who is a friend. This is a networking opportunity for both of us; therefore, eating to the side and a quick hello wouldn't be considered rude. I explain my predicament and suggest that we each get a plate of food and a drink and head off to a corner where we can talk and eat. Never make this person feel used. Be sure it is someone whom you see often and whose calls you return immediately and vice versa. Catch up on some pertinent news; then agree that after 5 to 10 minutes that it's time for both of you to get up and move around the room.

> *Summary: Determine what your priority is and give it your full attention. And always eat before you arrive at a stand-up event—no matter what the hour.*

How to Juggle a Glass and a Plate of Hors d'Oeuvres

First, I strongly suggest that you choose one or the other and not juggle. You will feel more confident, and that puts those around you at ease. If you must juggle, be very careful. Here are some guidelines:

- Stand near a table so that you can put your glass down frequently.
- Hold your glass in your left hand. Cold drinks in glasses and cans will sweat. If you are holding the drink in your

right hand and you reach out to shake hands, you will give the other person a cold, clammy handshake. Or you will have to do a "hipslap handshake" by wiping off the drink sweat on your clothes prior to shaking hands.

- When drinking white wine, hold your glass by the stem. This keeps your hand from warming the drink.
- Maintain eye contact when talking with someone.
- If you drop something in someone's home, pick it up immediately.
- If you are at a function, use your best judgment.
- Purchase a Party Clip that clips on your plate and has a ring to hold the wine glass (www.PartyClip.com).

"I Drink to Make Others More Interesting"

Networking frequently includes a bar. Today it is more socially acceptable not to drink at all, or at least to drink less. Whatever your tolerance is, know it and follow it. Some people get sleepy if they are tired and have a glass of wine on an empty stomach. You want to be unforgettable; however, there are some memories that are better than others.

Here are some thoughts:

- Alternate one alcoholic drink and one glass of water.
- Have a glass of seltzer with a splash of wine rather than the opposite.
- Consider stopping at two alcoholic drinks.
- If you don't drink, find a moment to tell the bartender what you prefer.
- Eat. This may sound simple, but it is easy to overlook. If you are hungry, don't risk your health or well-being by not getting some nourishment. Consider snacking ahead of time

or having a nutrition bar in your briefcase so that you are focused on networking, not on your stomach.

- Carry a snack in your briefcase, so that it's easy to have a few bites before you start drinking.
- Give up your car keys if they are requested.
- If you are in a home with light-colored carpet, stay with white wine or light-colored drinks.

Drinking from the Can

The reason you shouldn't do this isn't just because of manners. If you or someone you know did a stint working in a supply room while you were in college, you may remember that in addition to the stacks of canned goods, there were also critters and their remnants. Clean off the top of a soda or beer can and pour the liquid into a glass—if not for you, then for those who are watching who may have had such a summer job.

> *Summary: Networking—either social or business—is about making connections with others for either personal or professional reasons. Drinking can be a part of that. Know your audience and know yourself. Be appropriate and comfortable.*

BUSINESS CARDS—QUALITY VERSUS QUANTITY!

I actually went to a networking event where a game called business card Olympics was played. The idea was to get as many cards as possible during a set period of time. It was miserable. I was quite sure that not everyone there wanted my card, and vice versa. If I wanted only names, I could buy a list.

One high-quality conversation makes an event worthwhile, in my opinion. In some cases it's with a person I've met before, but we haven't done business together. Stick to your core goal of meeting people that you can add value to and vice versa. Remember, it's quality, not quantity, that counts.

AVOID CONVERSATIONS IN PUBLIC PLACES

There are reporters in elevators, sitting next to you at breakfast or in sessions, or standing in restrooms. There are also your competitors. Do *not* engage in any conversation in public that you do not wish to read about the next day in the paper or say anything that your CEO would rather that your competitors not know. You don't want to be the one to disclose trade secrets.

HOW TO MEET THE SPEAKER OR A VIP

Often we attend a meeting, event, or conference so that we can meet the speaker or a VIP who is also attending the session. After the person speaks, however, there is often a crowd, and it may be all but impossible to meet her. If you do truly want to meet such a person, first be sure that you have a specific goal. For example, you want to tell the speaker how much you like his book or to find out who in her company makes purchasing decisions on computers.

Consider approaching the person before he speaks. This means that you need to do some research in advance of the event. Go to the person's Web site and read the bio. Come up with a few questions you can ask. This way, if you find yourself in the elevator with the speaker prior to the presentation, you have a few moments to make a connection.

Speak for only a few minutes. If your goal is to get a meeting, then say so, explain why the person should make time for you, and move on. During a presentation, someone said that she wanted to meet the chairman of a large company. When she was asked for a few more details, it became clear that the chairman wasn't the right person at all. It is easy to think that the person at the top is the only one who can help you. In fact, ask who the right person is. This sends a message of respect and indicates that you are a true professional.

TALK TO PEOPLE WHO ARE ALONE

We all remember that feeling in high school when we were new and didn't know anyone to talk to. Now that we are adults, only the scene is different, and for some the feelings are just as painful. Approach people who are on their own. Before too long you can quickly form your own group that is having a brilliant conversation.

If the discussion is less thrilling than you'd like, consider it as a great chance to practice some new skills. In many cases, it is the first time the person has been to an event with the hosting organization. Introduce him to someone who is involved with the association. It gives you a chance to increase your visibility as well.

GET AN INTRODUCTION

If there is someone at the event that you specifically want to meet, find someone who can introduce you. This makes the entire situation less awkward. Consider sending an e-mail in advance to the person whom you would like to make the introduction. Articulate what you can offer the other person.

The Rolling Stones were featured on the September 30, 2002, cover of *Fortune*.[3] It turns out that their manager, Michael Cohl, is a very good networker. First of all, he knew his goal. Cohl "would produce new streams of revenue by selling skyboxes, bus tours, TV deals, and taking merchandise to a new level. He would bring in corporate sponsors like Volkswagen and Tommy Hilfiger."

Second, he knew who could help him execute the deal, Prince Rupert. But there was one problem: he didn't know the prince. So he networked until he found someone who did, and that was the band members from Pink Floyd. He called them and asked for an introduction.

Now before you pick up the phone and start asking for introductions, here's why Prince Rupert returned Cohl's call. When Rupert got the message from Pink Floyd, he trusted their judgment. He called Cohl and heard a compelling offer: "$40 million for 40 shows."

If you are in college and beginning your first job search, asking for an information interview is fine. However, later in life, you need to do your homework and learn as much as you possibly can about the other person. When the introduction is made, the person already wants to meet you.

When you are at an event and a chance presents itself, quickly ask yourself whether this will be your only opportunity to meet the other person. Be strategic, but don't be foolish. You want to come across as poised and polished, not ill prepared or opportunistic.

ASK WHAT YOU CAN DO FOR PEOPLE

When you meet someone you like and want to help, ask that person what you can do for her. (See the section "How to Ask for Help," in Chapter 12.) I find that just asking enhances the rapport with the other person. If you offer, be sure you do it. It is of little benefit to your reputation if you make offers and do not follow up.

FOLLOW UP

At the end of the XPlane document (see Figure 10-1), you see a "Lego Diane" walking out with business cards. This is where the rubber hits the road. Few people follow up at all, and even fewer know *how* to follow up. This is so important that it has its own chapter in the book. Read Chapter 11 carefully. If you fail to follow up, you have done yourself, your company, or your organization a serious disservice.

HOW TO RUN A NETWORKING EVENT OR MEETING

Much of *The Networking Survival Guide* is focused on you as the attendee or initiator of a networking situation. In many cases, however, you and your company will be expected to host events rather than attend them. This can be a fabulous moment for you and your firm to shine. It can also be your worst nightmare if a competent person isn't responsible for each detail.

It's risky to assume that your executive assistant can double as a meeting planner unless he has been specifically trained in this. Consider outsourcing the meeting or having your assistant work with someone in your organization who has handled events before. Some firms have a meeting planning department. Get in touch with this department as early as possible, and let it take care of all the event details.

When you work with a professional meeting planning department or firm, you can stay focused on your business needs and let someone else handle the details of the meeting. I contacted Meeting Planners International (MPI) for some suggestions. Here are some suggestions.

- *Hire a meeting planner who understands the importance of strategy.* It is important that the planner understand the goals, the audience, the history of past event successes and failures, the budget parameters, and the client's expectations.

- *Clearly define the goals and objectives of the event.* Defining these expectations will ensure that you focus the proper amount of attention on the appropriate event elements. Your return on investment (ROI) is an important outcome of the event that will be determined by measurable goals.

- *Select a location that will appeal to your attendees.* The event location will make or break your event, for a couple of reasons. Whether you choose to hold your event in a hotel, a museum, a boat, or a historic mansion, the location should reflect the type of event you wish to create and should be desirable to your guests.

- *Remember to leave time for networking.* Too often, enthusiasm for creating the event gets the better of you, and you pack too much into a short period of time. Leave ample time for guests to meet and mingle with one another over drinks or food, or follow a stage presentation with a networking reception.

- *Help others to meet one another.* One of the best ways to assist people in networking with one another is to have members of your event team or staff assist in the person-to-person introductions.[4]

I have great respect for the myriad of details that meeting planners manage. From my experience attending many functions, here are a few key thoughts:

- *Hold a pre-event meeting.* Schedule a time when everyone who will be at the event can get together. Be sure that everyone knows the purpose of the event, who the attendees are, and what is expected of company representatives.

- *Discuss expected employee behavior.* It's ridiculous to attend a hosted event and find clusters of employees whispering and frantically hanging on to each other as if they were in high school. Your employees must be confident and capable of walking up to anyone and representing the company. If they don't know someone, they should introduce themselves and indicate their role in the organization. If they can't do this, send them home. They will damage your firm's reputation.

- *Teach handshakes.*
- *Make sure that everyone who is at the event knows and can say what your company does and whom you serve.*
- *Review what is considered confidential information.* Use some examples: "If someone at the party asks what our sales to date are, introduce them to Jeff Smith in sales, and he can answer the question."
- *Remove confidential information from walls.* An event attendee told me she once went to a competitor's party and saw the quarterly numbers on a wall chart.
- *Have name badges printed ahead of time.* Place them in alphabetical order facing the guests. Be sure they are readable. Do not use the ones that hang around someone's neck, forcing people to "belly button scan" for names.
- *Serve food that is easy to eat standing up.*
- *Create buffer time in the schedule.* This allows people time to relax, make phone calls, and check e-mail.
- *Be sure it is clear who will follow up with leads.* For about three months after I attended an event, I had two or three people from the same company calling me. It was never clear why each person was calling. The only thing that was clear was that each was on commission.
- *Send yourself or your assistant to a meeting planning class if you cannot afford to hire a meeting planner.*
- *Familiarize yourself with Robert's Rules of Order[5] before hosting a meeting.*

Social Networking Isn't for the Unsmiling: Jeff Cutler

Jeff Cutler, a social media journalist, shared his thoughts with me on the sincerity that each person's network is built upon:

The best way I've been able to build my contact list and develop more of a following, both online and IRL (in real life), is by being genuine in my interactions and by spending time with people.

This time can be broken down into time on Twitter, Facebook, LinkedIn, and the blogs that people maintain. I also contribute to my own series of blogs and a video show as a way to share my thoughts and time with people.

Essentially, I try to make my brand—JeffCutler.com—a resource for others to leverage. Be it on a personal or a community level, I've found that by sharing my knowledge freely, I get returns that are 10- to 100-fold in scope.

Here are two examples:

For months I've been attending a community roundtable discussion in Harvard Square, Cambridge, Massachusetts. There, I contribute my thoughts on building teams, communicating with audiences, empathizing with clients and colleagues, and crafting effective messages.

This participation hadn't borne any fruit until recently, when I met a person who hired me to help her reach a community of people using the same approach. She wanted to know how I came to be such an "expert," and I said that most of it is just showing up.

Second, I've been a journalist for two decades. I've used that time to build up relationships with organizations that use my skills in traditional ways. But now I've been asked to contribute in new ways (as a resource on social media for the media trainer). This never would have occurred if I hadn't put in the time and effort to forge and maintain relationships.

Just being at events, smiling and shaking hands, returning e-mails promptly, participating in online groups, and making yourself a resource is more valuable than you can measure. Especially as more interaction is being done with a foot in both pools—online and IRL.

11

Follow-Up Techniques

Networking is a recurring commitment.
> ~ PAM ALEXANDER, Alexander & Ogilvy

The difference between successful networking and unsuccessful networking is follow-up. Few people do this at all, much less do it well. *Follow-up* means that you are interested in further developing a positive relationship for both parties. It is also important that you imagine yourself on the other side of the table. When people follow up with you, answer their request or call. None of us likes to say no to anyone; however, when we return someone's calls even if we don't have the answer that that person wants, we are sending a signal that we are professionals who treats others well.

This chapter will provide techniques, resources, technology shortcuts, and much more. It will cover how to follow up online and by e-mail, voice mail, and snail mail, and which one to use in what situation.

WHICH METHOD TO USE WHEN

How you follow up is determined by the urgency of the situation. If you are moving quickly into a sales mode and you want to close the business, then make that determination and proceed accordingly. Send an express package with contracts or e-mail pertinent information.

If you are following up for networking (e.g., to say thank you, identify the next steps, or stay in touch), then you want to pick the right channel for the person and the situation. If possible, when you are communicating with the person, ask how he prefers to be contacted.

If you are following up with a Facebook or LinkedIn invitation, here are a few guidelines:

- Ask the person whether she is on LinkedIn or Facebook and whether she is open to invitations on those services. In many business networking situations, a new contact may have a company fan page on Facebook in addition to a personal profile. For example, I have two Facebook pages— one for personal and one for business. In every case, take advantage of the ability to personalize your message instead of quickly sending the template request that the services provide.
- If we knew each other growing up, had a cup of coffee, and talked about life, goals, and other such issues, then invite me personally at www.Facebook.com/DianeDarling. This means that I will be likely to recognize your name when I see the invitation.
- If you've seen me speak, read my book, or want to know when or where I'm speaking, then connect with me on www.Facebook.com/EffectiveNetworking.

Use e-mail when time is absolutely of the essence, but your voice/tone isn't. For example, you are giving someone directions to a meeting the next day, or you are introducing two people to each other. Alternatively, use voice mail when the energy of your voice is important. If by chance there was a misunderstanding, the kind tone of your voice may make it less of a problem.

You can *never* go wrong using snail mail. I've never heard anyone complain about receiving a handwritten thank-you note. Of course, the contents may have been too pushy—for example, it may have been sent with an unrequested brochure. I suggest that you drop a note in the mail whenever you possibly can. It sends a message that you are a thoughtful person, and it certainly differentiates you from many others who simply type an e-mail. It takes a few extra minutes, and that's what is noticed.

Ask the person what he prefers when you follow up. Some people definitely have a preference. If so, use that method!

Summary: Urgency and efficiency are determining factors when following up.

"CAN I BUY YOU LUNCH?"

If you invite someone to lunch, be clear about what you want. If you are looking for advice or you want to tap into the person's expertise, it may not be the best approach. In essence, you are buying an hour or more of this person's consulting time for not much money and taking her away from her work. Unless you know the individual well, it can come across as presumptuous and almost insulting. I've even had clients share horror stories with me about someone inviting them to lunch and then expecting to split the bill.

Summary: Time expires—once it's spent, it's gone. People guard it carefully and value it highly. If you do so as well, your networking efforts will be recognized, appreciated, and reciprocated.

IF NOT LUNCH, WHAT TO ASK FOR?

Give someone an option that he can say yes to (and make it easy to do so). For example, suggest coffee for 15 minutes at the person's office. Personally, I almost never say yes to lunch. I prefer to take a break from work, and I like to connect with someone on a social basis rather than through work. A busy professional is more likely to be able to fit you into the calendar for coffee, not to mention that his assistant and phone are nearby. On occasions, the person I'm visiting has picked up the phone and introduced me immediately.

"Coffee dates" involve less of a time commitment and are seen as less intrusive than a lunch meeting. Plus there's less risk of having a conversation with a valuable contact with a sesame seed stuck in your teeth!

Let the person know why you want to meet and what you are asking for. You will significantly increase your chances of getting her time and attention. Once I e-mailed someone and asked if he knew a certain person and would be willing to make an introduction. He wrote back and said of course he knew this person, but he needed to know why I wanted to contact the other person before he would use his connections.

> *Summary: Think about what will get the other person to say yes. Ask for that!*

MAKE IT POSSIBLE, AND COMFORTABLE, FOR THE PERSON TO SAY NO

While most of us don't like the word *no*, it does provide an answer. If the person feels that she can say no, she will respect you. When you ask for something in the future, that will be duly remembered. Say thank you and move on.

> *Summary: Stalkers are not good networkers.*

AFTER YOU ARE INTRODUCED

If someone made an introduction on your behalf and the new contact is not returning calls, here are some tips on what to do next:

- Call the person who made the introduction and let him know that you are not getting a response.
- Ask for advice on what the next steps should be.
- Always update that person on the status of the new connection. It's polite, it makes the person feel appreciated, and it gives you a valid excuse to be in touch.

Summary: Keep the person who made the introduction informed of the status.

THREE STRIKES AND YOU ARE OUT

I'm frequently asked how many times someone should follow up. Switch places and ask yourself how many times you want someone to contact you. You want to be known as someone who is respectful and businesslike. Keep these tips in mind as you attempt to solidify your new connections:

- *Before* you follow up, be sure you know the best way (her preference, not yours!) to connect with the person.
- Rarely do I follow up more than three times.
- I start out with both an e-mail and a phone call with a clear, thoughtful, organized message. (See the section "Voice Mail," in Chapter 12.)
- Write out your voice mail message and rehearse it *out loud* before you call. Be prepared to have a conversation if the person answers the phone! Sometimes I answer my phone, and it's clear from the caller's tongue-tied response that he was expecting to get my voice mail. Use technology,

don't hide behind it! Be ready to ask for the business, the contribution, or the job.

- Make sure your e-mail message has an attention-getting subject line. Keep it short, and be very clear about what you are requesting.

- If there's no response to those contact attempts, I go back to the person who made the introduction (see the previous section). If she advises me to keep trying, I will leave one more voice mail message. However, some friends have told me about an alternative that works well for them. It's an old salesman's technique called "pyramiding," and it applies primarily to telephone contacts. The first day, you make four calls but leave only one message. (See the section "The Difference between Persistence and Stalking" below. The following day, you make three attempts. Then two, and then finally one. The person gets a single message each day. If you don't reach that person, you can be satisfied that you made your best effort.

- Sometimes people do reject us, but they forget to tell us so. Well, they actually do tell us, but they do it in their own way. They don't return our calls or respond to our e-mails. On the other hand, remember "the law of relative priority." *Our* top priority—speaking with that person—is unlikely to be at the top of that person's to-do list. We have to tread the fine line between being persistent enough and being *too* persistent.

Summary: Learn when to put your energy elsewhere.

THE DIFFERENCE BETWEEN PERSISTENCE AND STALKING

While the difference is subtle, once you fall into the stalking category, it can be difficult, if not impossible, to maneuver back.

- *Persistence* is perseverance, determination, and resolution.
- *Stalking* is pestering, annoying, aggravating; a synonym can even be persecution.

It is gratifying when people are enthusiastic about working with us or providing services and products. However, it can be unnerving when they cross that invisible line. Instead of being someone that we would like to work with in the future, such a person shifts to being a part of a network of people to avoid.

Esther Dyson, author and chair of ED Ventures, a global information service company, shared a story. When she was at a trade show in Las Vegas, she was swimming laps. At the end of her lane was someone who had come to the pool and was waiting for her. He strongly suggested that she stop by his company's booth at the show.

This type of behavior can quickly lead to the demise of a professional or personal relationship. At that point, it is best to let go, note the lessons learned, and start over.

Summary: Proper follow-up can lead to a successful long-term business or personal relationship. Improper follow-up will guarantee that your efforts now and in the future are likely to be wasted.

12

Best Practices when You Are
Not Face-to-Face

Given what you know now about the power of body language, it is always preferable to be face-to-face with a networking contact. Your goal should be to get your "face in the place" whenever possible. However, that isn't always possible. Here are some techniques to help you maximize your networking opportunities when being there just isn't an option and to ensure that when you *do* meet in person, you are fully prepared.

ONLINE

The most familiar names in online networking sites are LinkedIn and Facebook. Twitter has emerged recently as another option in the online arena. Which should you use? It depends mostly on your comfort level. Kate Brodock, founder of marketing consultancy the Other Side Group, is an expert on helping business and nonprofit clients use online social networks. She presents frequently to groups on social media, including their use as a networking resource.

Kate identifies three keys to the effective use of online networking services:

- *Research* is where you learn about companies and individuals.
- *Personal branding* is the corollary to this component and describes the process by which you ensure that people and companies learning about you get an accurate and positive picture.
- *Networking* is where the two parties come together to interact and confirm or refute the preconceived image that each has of the other.

As you can see in Figure 12-1, the major social networking sites are involved throughout this process. LinkedIn is helpful in learning about the more professional aspects of individuals and organizations; an individual's or company's Twitter presence can also yield insights into personality and culture. LinkedIn (and if you want, a personal or professional blog) can help create your personal brand by establishing credentials and expertise; a carefully managed Facebook account provides a look at your more personal side. All three sites can provide opportunities for online networking. *One cautionary note:* you have the networking channels that you prefer, both online and offline. Don't be surprised or offended if a new contact doesn't share those preferences! The beauty of these new online resources is that it increases the possibility that you will have a shared preference.

More and more networking is done, or at least initiated, online. In fact, according to one expert, online is the primary and preferred networking channel for people under 35. Dianne Durkin is the president and founder of Loyalty Factor, LLC, which consults with corporations to help them build and maintain loyalty with their workforce and customers. Dianne has done extensive research on generational differences in communication and work styles. According to Dianne,

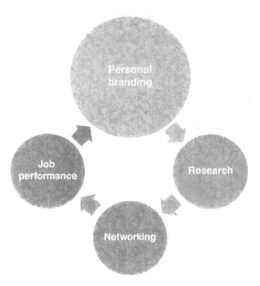

Figure 12-1   Research, Personal Branding, and Networking

"the [baby] boomers' experience is generally with face-to-face networking however many are becoming familiar with LinkedIn and Facebook for social and business contacts. Younger people are quite comfortable initiating and maintaining relationships online, and often prefer it."[1]

Whatever your age or experience level, you should be familiar with online networking tools or risk missing valuable opportunities to make and develop useful contacts. If you are unfamiliar with LinkedIn, for example, and you are nervous about "doing it right," Durkin has some reassuring advice. "People using social media," she reports, "want to help each other."

The following sections examine the primary social networking sites in more detail. Remember, these are just the biggest and most general sites. If you have a hobby, a specialized interest, or specific expertise, there is almost certainly an online community dedicated to it. Interacting with people in that community can help to broaden your personal and professional network. Explore sites like Ning.com, or try Yahoo! groups to find like-minded folks who will appreciate your insights on macramé, fly-tying, or numismatics.

LinkedIn

The most familiar name to those using social media for professional networking is LinkedIn.com. Founded in 2003, the service ended 2008 with 33 million members. Another advantage of LinkedIn for networkers is that members are more willing to connect than those on more socially oriented sites like Facebook or MySpace. As you enter your work history and education, LinkedIn will show other employees at those companies and alumni from those institutions who are on LinkedIn. You can even check to see if contacts in your Outlook, Gmail, or Yahoo! address books are on LinkedIn (don't worry, they won't spam your contacts). It is in the service's interest to be as useful as possible, and the best way to do that is to help members expand their networks quickly.

Once you have started to create a LinkedIn network, then what? Suppose you see a posting for a position with Company A. You'd like to apply for the job, but you know that thousands of other people could be seeing the same post and applying, too. How can you get the inside track? Enter the name of the firm in LinkedIn. You will see a list of people at Company A to whom you are connected in some way. These are presented as first-degree (you are connected to them), second-degree (one of your connections knows them), and third-degree (one of your connections knows one of their connections) contacts. Someone you already know or one of his connections is in a position to help you!

As you'd expect, introduction requests are very common on LinkedIn. From a networking perspective, it is important to remember that just because you *can* easily see a connection to someone you want to meet does not mean that you *should* ask your connection for a referral! Stop first and think whether the value you can offer to the third person is apparent. You wouldn't want to expend your "social capital" on a frivolous introduction, so don't expect your connections to feel differently. However, if you do believe you can provide value, don't be fazed if your connection is not a close one. Recall Dianne Durkin's earlier comment—people using social media want to help each other.

Back in Chapter 3, I introduced the idea of *hybrid networking.* Particularly in a case where the connection to the person you want is not current (a college buddy you haven't seen in a while; an employee from another department at a company you worked for several years ago), take the opportunity to strengthen that connection as you pursue that referral! Call the person to catch up or, if she's local, ask to meet for coffee. That way, asking for the referral will be less "out of the blue," and the referral will probably be much stronger.

In closing, LinkedIn is also home to a plethora of group forums on various business topics. Join one and get a sense for the discussions that go on. Once you get comfortable and you see a topic on which you want to give your opinion, chime in! This can result in other group members introducing themselves and more additions to your network. You can also answer business questions posed by other members—a great way to build credibility and attract connections with other LinkedIn users.

Summary: Think 'business attire' when networking on LinkedIn.

Facebook

Facebook makes it incredibly easy to connect (or reconnect) with family and friends. High school friends who haven't spoken in a decade can be catching up and sharing recent family photos within minutes of joining. This ease of connection and sharing is the biggest reason for Facebook's success. Members can share photos, video, songs, and games; the Facebook platform can accommodate every type of content. With all this sharing, however, come some risks for members hoping to use the site for networking.

One of the biggest risks for those using Facebook to advance themselves professionally is inappropriate content. Whether it's photos from that Club Med trip you took last summer or an ill-considered late-night rant about the company that just laid you off, it is easy to find Facebook "horror stories" of socially and/or professionally damaging material that came back to haunt some members. Many employers now run the names of job candidates on the social networking sites. The actual risk is not that high, and Facebook's privacy settings allow members to allow different levels of access to different subsets of friends (family members versus college buddies versus professional contacts, for example). Still, if it's a concern, it's probably a good idea to make your personal profile private except to close friends and family members.

If you are networking to promote a business venture and you are eager to leverage Facebook's rich media-sharing capabilities, there's some good news. Facebook's developers have made enormous strides in 2009 toward making the service more business friendly. Even better for those concerned about keeping their personal lives private, Facebook now allows businesses and organizations to establish a presence independent of the creator's personal profile. "Facebook pages" (also called "Fan Pages," a holdover from an early version of the functionality) let businesses promote events, hold contests, and post company news.

Go to the "resources" area at http://effectivenetworking.com to learn how you can create a page for your company. Mine is www. Facebook.com/EffectiveNetworking—please feel free to become a fan and post comments about this book!

Summary: Think khakis or 'casual' when networking on Facebook. Mind you that doesn't mean …. "naked, vulgar, or inappropriate."

Twitter

Twitter has received a lot of attention recently. Celebrities like Oprah and Ellen DeGeneres are now using the site, and millions of people have joined them to explore the often mystifying 140-character world. Journalists and conference attendees have found Twitter messages (called "tweets") to be valuable in reporting events as they happen. Charities have leveraged the viral power of "retweets" (forwarding a message to your network) to find new supporters and contributions. Twitter messages often include links to Web sites, with the message serving as a headline or teaser to draw viewers to explore further.

Unlocking the power of Twitter is similar to finding success using most of the tools and techniques in this book. The key is building a network of people whose expertise you value and to whom you can offer value. Go to search.twitter.com and enter a few terms on a subject that is personally or professionally interesting to you. You will see a list of tweets containing that term. You will see that many contain links to additional relevant material contained in other, longer-form data sources. Click on the authors of the messages that you find most interesting or useful. By "following" or subscribing to these users, you will start to build a Twitter network. You can then restrict the messages you see to those from and directed to the users you follow—a far more manageable and useful solution.

Don't feel compelled to post your own tweets immediately. Do a search in Twitter for a topic that interests you, and click on the authors of tweets that you like. On the author's page, you will see a button to follow that person. You will then see all that person's messages. Listen for a while to develop an ear for the exchanges. You might want to start by simply retweeting messages that you find useful. Then jump in!

It may seem incongruous at first to hear these collections of slang, abbreviations, and compressed URLs described as "conversations." Yet that is what they are. Individuals—friends or colleagues, online acquaintances, even strangers—are using Twitter for asking and answering questions, arranging meetings, recruiting new employees, and myriad other purposes.

Used correctly, Twitter can be a wonderful resource for networking. Here as elsewhere, however, it is important to remember that networking is not the same as simply asking for something. In some cases you might get it, but real value is found in building relationships from which each party derives some benefit.

> *Summary: Twitter works for some and not others. Test it and then decide.*

PERSONAL WEB SITES

With the growing popularity of online networking, it can be helpful to have a place to which you can direct people who want to learn more about you. A personal Web site can be comparable to that of a company, but it certainly doesn't have to be. The popularity of the social networking sites previously described shows that people want to interact, and your site should accommodate that desire.

A lot of people who want to get online start with a blog. If you have a personal or professional passion, why not share it? There are several sites that will host your creation for free, providing templates and other tools. Or you can go "self-hosted," where you purchase a domain name (about $10 a year) and pay a small fee (as low as $3 to $4 a month) to a hosting company. If you think this will be a long-term project, you are probably better off hosting your own blog—this will provide flexibility for expansion in the future. Here are some other tips:

1. Purchase your own name (DianeDarling.com) or something that you can use professionally.
2. Create your Web site. This doesn't have to be long; two or three pages is fine.
   a. *Hosted:* Blogspot, Wordpress.com.

b. *Self-hosted:* Typepad, Wordpress.org (separate from Wordpress.com!).

    c. *Standard site:* Webs.com and Weebly.com are just two of the plethora of companies that make creating a site as easy as filling in a form. Many are free to use and will host your site, as well.

3. Be professional, even with any personal information you share.

4. Keep it current. It is far worse to have a Web site that has not been updated in months than not to have one!

5. Be sure that the material can be printed without going off the page (portrait format).

6. Have contact information on every page.

7. Don't use your home phone number—have a separate line that children and other family members won't be answering.

8. Don't use your home address.

Summary: Creating a personal Web site can be very helpful in marketing yourself. It is easy and inexpensive to "stake your claim" online, but remember that making your site interesting does require an ongoing commitment of time.

E-MAIL

E-mail is a very useful tool that has revolutionized the way we communicate. For some, it's the best invention since the wheel. For others, it's the collapse of civilization, grammar, and spelling. As with any form of communication, it is wise to take a few minutes and ask yourself if it is the best way to communicate your specific message. There is nothing right or wrong about e-mail as a technology. How it is used is what matters. Take these items into consideration:

- As you sit down to compose a message, first ask yourself if e-mail is the best method of communication for this message. Don't forfeit 93 percent of your communication power if you don't have to. If you are giving someone driving directions, e-mail is ideal. If you are expressing yourself, you can be misunderstood fast.

- Make sure you know that e-mail is a method that the person you are trying to reach uses. If the answer is yes, then follow a few guidelines to ensure maximum impact.

- Think of your message as a postcard. The information can be interrupted, forwarded, or edited. Be sure that this is the best way to communicate. If the recipient chooses to forward it, how will that affect you and your business/career?

Your Name/E-mail Address

- Make sure that your e-mail software is set up so that your name is visible to the receiver.

- People are looking at their inbox for your name, not your e-mail address.

- Consider including your phone number in your settings. For example, when I send an e-mail, it comes from "Diane Darling | 617.247.2700".

- If you are unsure of how to set this up, go to the Help section of your e-mail program. For example, for Outlook, go to Inbox, then Tools, then click e-mail accounts.

- Business e-mail should use a professional e-mail address. People may not remember that your e-mail address is susan-jones@hotmail.com. But they will likely remember Diane@DianeDarling.com.

Subject Line

- Think of this as a headline. Imagine looking at a newspaper or magazine and skimming the headlines. That's what the other person should see when she sees the inbox. As the person is reviewing the "headlines," give her a reason to read your e-mails.
- In some cases, you can actually communicate the entire message in the subject line
- If the entire conversation takes place in the subject line, the only reason to open the message would be to get the other person's contact information.

CC

This should be used when everyone on the list knows everyone else, everyone has explicitly or implicitly given permission to have his e-mail address broadcast, and the e-mail does not contain any confidential material. An example would be directions to a meeting or event, the agenda for a meeting, or event details.

BCC

- Always use this when an e-mail is sent to a large group.
- Put your name and e-mail address in the "to" line and all the other e-mail addresses in the "BCC" line.
- Use BCC when those on the list would not want their e-mail addresses shared publicly. For example, use it for an announcement of a new e-mail address or new job information.
- When in doubt, use BCC.

Bullets

People read their e-mail quickly. Consider using a bullet format, which provides an easy way for people to read the message. *Note*: This works only with HTML e-mail, not text. With text, use hyphens instead.

!—Important

What you consider important, the recipient may not. Use the important flag (exclamation point) prudently.

Reply

E-mail is often sent back and forth. Typically other subjects get added in, and before you know it the subject is completely different. Change the subject line when the reply message is about a new topic.

Signature

You wouldn't send out a letter without a signature; the same is true for e-mail. At the bottom of each e-mail should be a "signature." You may want to have several versions. At a minimum, include your name and phone number. Otherwise, add your title, the name of your company, your Web site, your e-mail address, contact information for your assistant, and all applicable phone numbers.

If you don't know how to create a signature, click on the help section of your e-mail service. It typically takes just a few steps, and once it's created, it is automatically included in each message.

Here's a sample signature:

Text of the message

Best, Diane

Diane Darling

617.247.2700 :: Office

Diane@EffectiveNetworking.com

Other

- Use proper grammar.
- Be aware that e-mail can easily be intercepted. I found this out the hard way when an e-mail complaining about my boss ended up being forwarded to her. Yikes!
- Know and follow the e-mail policies at your office.
- Mis-sent e-mail can have legal implications.
- Never send an angry e-mail.
- Watch the clock. If you send business e-mail at all hours of the night, you could be signaling that you are not a good time manager.
- If there is any possibility that your e-mail could be misinterpreted, set up a phone appointment instead.

Summary: Using professional e-mail techniques can facilitate and accelerate a business relationship.

PHONE

"More than 75 percent of new contacts make their decision about whether or not to do further business with you during the initial phone call."[2]

Guidelines for Making Calls

- Know what you want and what you are going to say or ask *before* the person answers the phone.
- Script your message.
- Rehearse it—out loud!
- Smile when you call.
- Whenever possible, try to get the person "live" rather than leaving a voice mail message.

Guidelines for Receiving Calls

- Answer calls by the third ring (at the latest).
- Smile when you answer the phone.
- Write down the caller's name immediately.
- Be available. I called a company that has a system where you say your name and then the person either takes the call or doesn't. After a few times, I could only assume that the person either didn't really work there or was avoiding my calls. Of course you feel rejected if someone doesn't take your call. Be present!
- Return calls within 48 hours.
- Use the person's name during the call.
- Make notes when you talk.
- Stand up if you have a problem paying attention.
- Turn your back to your computer.
- Thank the person for calling.

Here's a fun story about a decision made by someone who understood how you come across on the phone. Sheila loved to talk to people and was excellent at her job. I mentioned that I had a new client for her. As I was on the phone, he walked by, so I said I'd transfer the call and connect them. "*No!*" she said. "I'm not dressed right." I laughed and said, "You must be kidding—you're on the phone." She explained that she feels better about herself when she is dressed in business attire, and at the moment she was in jeans. It wasn't how she wanted to "meet" a potential new customer.

Summary: Are you dressed for your call?

VOICE MAIL

Once, when I listened to my voice mail, there was a message with a name that I didn't know. The phone number was said so fast that only "Rain Man" could have figured it out. He also gave his e-mail address (spoken as fast as an NFL pass as well). The more I hit replay, the more aggravated I got. I never did figure out the phone number or the e-mail address. Instead, I had to call the person's boss to find out what was going on, which was aggravating for everyone.

We are networking all the time. Each time we connect with someone, we are either reinforcing the positive image he has of us or beginning to contribute to his impression that we may not be that brilliant after all.

Before you call or e-mail, take a brief moment to ask yourself if the call is necessary. Are you calling because it is easier to ask someone else to do your work? One time I got a call from someone asking for the phone number of a company. Whether or not this was true, she came across as lazy.

Summary: Before you pick up the phone to ask a data question, try to find the information elsewhere. Make contact with someone when you are providing information, not asking for something you already have or can get elsewhere.

How to Leave a Voice Mail Message

Voice mail is a reality in our world. The technology is not going to go away. Learn to make it your friend and an effective networking tool. What happens is that we naturally get nervous, get tongue-tied, and ramble.

Summary: Learn how to leave voice mail. This is a communication tool that can provide a positive image to the recipient or a negative one. The choice is yours. Practice your message. If you can review it before finalizing it, do so.

Follow these guidelines to use voice mail effectively:

Prepare
- Write down what you want to say. It doesn't need to be word for word; even bullet points will help you.
- If you tend to get nervous, write *calm down* on an index card and breathe.
- Because I know I can talk fast, I often write "S-L-O-W D-O-W-N" on a piece of paper.
- Make a connection with the other person as early in the message as possible. Here are some things to be sure you say:
  - Who referred you
  - The purpose of the call
  - Your name
  - Your phone number and/or e-mail address
  - The best time or way to reach you
  - Your name and contact information again

Practice
One of my favorite television programs of late is *Grey's Anatomy*, in part because the dialogue is so compelling—it sounds as if the cast members have just said their lines off the top of their heads. It sounds real and genuine. Actors are highly paid to make us believe

something, and business professionals can take the cue. If you don't like feeling as if you are acting, then consider it "rehearsed spontaneity." The entire reason for you to practice is to gain confidence and come across in a compelling and professional manner. Here are some ideas:

- Say the message out loud a few times.
- If you stumble over a certain part, practice it over and over again.
- Start with the person's name, if possible. For example, if you are calling John because Bob recommended that you do so, start with, "John, Bob recommended that I give you a call."
- Call your own voice mail and record the message.
- Play it back. Is it a message that the person will listen to?
- *Very important:* When you leave your phone number, picture the person on the other end of the phone looking for a piece of paper, then searching for a pen. If you give your phone number too fast, this will significantly decrease the odds of your call's being returned.

Content

Even if you leave a clear message with a phone number that the person can write down and a name that she can spell, if the message isn't compelling, it's doubtful that you'll get a call back. Here is a sample message to give you an idea of what you should say.

- If you were referred by someone, start there: "Your attorney, Mr. Smith, suggested that I contact you." If my attorney asked someone to contact me, I'd keep listening.
- "He mentioned that you were looking for a Web designer to help on a new project." You are immediately a problem solver—*not* just trying to sell your Web designing services.

- "I'd be very interested in talking with you about the project. [Pause!] My name is Susan Jones, and I can be reached in a few ways." You are now preparing the person to find a piece of paper and pen.

- "I can be reached at 617-555-1212." Say each digit separately. It's not "twelve twelve," it's "one, two, one, two." Always leave your phone number. If it's not on the piece of paper that the person is holding, the person doesn't have it!

- Make it easy for people to stay connected with you. "I'll also give you my e-mail address if that would be a better way for us to connect. I can be reached at susanjones@ yahoo.com."

- If there is something that needs to be explained, such as spelling or punctuation, say so. If your name rhymes with or sounds like something, use that as a way to be memorable and clear. For example, the people who sit near my office probably hear in their sleep, "Diane with one *n* and Darling like sweetheart."

- Your goal is to get a return call.

- Be personable and professional.

The message needs to provide enough specific information to let the person know what should happen next. For example, if you are reconfirming a meeting, say your name, the purpose of the call, the details of the meeting, and the way the person can contact you if there is a change; then thank him and give him your contact info.

Here are some questions to ask yourself:

- Did you leave your contact information clearly at the beginning and end of the call?

- Is the receiver informed of what you do and why she should care?

- Does the receiver know what's expected of him—a phone call, an e-mail, or something else?

- Does the receiver know what to expect from you?
- How would you rate your energy?

How to Get Your Calls Returned

When you are a sincere person with a valid question or idea, it's frustrating when you make a call, and your call isn't returned. You will increase your chances by following a few guidelines:

- Return all your calls. While others may not do so, really do your best and then try a little harder. Get the universe on your side.
- Make it clear what you are asking.
- Leave your phone number.
- Call during working hours. I find it unnerving when I get messages during off hours. Why not call me when I'm likely to be at my desk?
- *Note:* There are two reasons that I don't return phone calls:
  - ○ The person didn't leave a phone number, so I don't have it on the piece of paper where I wrote down the message.
  - ○ I lost the piece of paper.
- Call again—you have three chances! Give the person the benefit of the doubt.

Summary: Well-structured voice mail messages provide a forum that allows the dialogue to continue. Use the technology to your benefit.

Your Outgoing Message

Here are some quick guidelines:

- If you don't like your voice, have someone else record the message. (You're welcome to call Effective Networking during off hours and listen to the recording: 617-247-2700.)
- Script the message.
- Change your message if you are on vacation or won't be able to return calls within a day or so.
- Let frequent callers know how they can bypass the message.
- Include another way to get in touch with you.
- Say the number s-l-o-w-l-y and spell out any unusual words.
- Speak slowly so that people can hear what you say.

MAKE A CALL OR TAKE YOUR CALL— THE CRUCIAL DIFFERENCE!

The reason most people don't like to make calls is that they are afraid of rejection. Human beings naturally want to be successful, and it is tedious to make calls and not get through. Thus, there is a crucial difference between making a call and having someone take your call.

You will significantly increase your chances of success if you set this up in advance as you are networking. Here are some ideas:

- Ask the person if it's okay for you to follow up.
- Find out the best way to do so, and suggest a phone call. You know the power of your voice; do what you can to maximize your chance of success.
- Ask if there are preferred times or days to call. Some people block off times where they don't take any calls.
- Get the name of the person's assistant.

Summary: There is a big difference between making a call and having someone take it. When you are networking, make a high-quality connection with the other person so that she will take your call.

SNAIL MAIL (A STAMP CAN MAKE THE DIFFERENCE)

Ask yourself how many e-mails you get a day. Now ask yourself how many handwritten thank-you notes you get.

We pay attention to handwritten notes because they are so rare. They get our attention. We save them at Effective Networking, Inc.

Put together a small envelope that includes note cards, stamps, and a pen. When you have finished a meeting (and certainly a job or information interview), sit in the lobby or your car and write a thank-you note. Put it in the mailbox. The satisfaction of completing the task is worth it. Be sure you do this within 24 hours.

Gents, this also applies to you! Get monogrammed note cards from a department store or a stationery store such as Crane's. I have received only a few handwritten business-related notes from men in my entire life, and I have them all.The thank-you note is not your life story, the reason someone should hire you, or why your product is the best. It is simply to thank someone for his time and to acknowledge that you appreciate his advice and ideas.

In all cases, include your business card with the thank-you note. Make it easy for the person to follow up with you.

Summary: A first-class stamp sends the message that you are indeed a first-class person!

HOW TO ASK FOR HELP! NETWORKING TO THE EXPONENTIAL POWER

You now know the importance of networking and making connections. Next, you need to ask people for help. Asking for help is hard for some people. It makes them feel weak or needy. What's really happening is that we think that other people can somehow read our minds and know what we need.

This became clear to me recently when I walked to the elevator in my apartment building. While I was waiting, I put on my gloves, hat, boots, and all that extra garb you need during the winter. The elevator didn't come, and I was getting frustrated. Then I realized what was wrong—I'd forgotten to hit the button. I laughed and realized that this is how I often treat people. I expect them to help me—but I forgot to tell them what I need. In this case it was a simple ride down to the lobby.

During our networking workshops, we make time for people to introduce themselves and pose a specific question to the group. For example, if someone is looking to meet a particular person in a company, that person may ask if anyone can facilitate an introduction. We call this $N\frac{x}{y}$.

Here are some examples:

- "I'd like to meet Mr. Jones at Top Drawer Computers. I'd like to explore a partnership. We offer strategic planning for medical device manufacturers."
- "We are seeking a new director of marketing. If you know of any qualified candidates, please let me know."
- "Our neighborhood is seeking two to three people to help with planting a garden. If you know of someone who would like to participate, have him or her call 555-1212."

It's hard to ask for help. We don't want to appear needy. We don't want to "bother" people. The result? We confuse a need with being needy. Then we hint.

Lily Tomlin is quoted as having said, "When I grow up, I want to be somebody. I guess I should have been more specific."

During this portion of the program for a group of women, someone said that she had a question, but it was a bit off-topic. "Go ahead and ask," I said.

"I really need a gold bag for a black-tie event on Saturday night." The hands shot up!

Her request was specific, so many people were able to help her. People could visualize what a gold bag looks like, we knew her deadline, and many of them had been to a black-tie event.

Tips for Offering and Asking for Help

Follow these tips when both offering and asking for help:

- When preparing for a networking call or event, be sure you have an answer if someone asks, "How can I help you?"
- Be as specific as you possibly can.
- If you are a job hunter, don't say, "I'm looking for something in software." Say "I want to contribute my skills to a software company, such as Computer Associates, in QA helping to deliver quality products."
  - *Note*: Depending on the forum, the term *QA* either will or will not make sense.
  - Be careful about using buzzwords or slang that will intimidate others and keep them from helping.
- Give the listener a few options.
- Position yourself as a problem solver or a people developer.
- When you are networking to increase your practice or business, be sure you can say what industry is your target market, who is the decision maker, and, most important, what problems you can solve.

Summary: When you ask for help, say it in such a way that someone can visualize the situation. This will greatly increase your chances of success.

Before you head out to network, ask yourself, if someone offers help, what will you say? An answer such as winning the lottery is dreamy; however, it is not necessarily professional. Be specific; say, "I've helped several companies reduce their time from concept to delivery, particularly in the medical industry. Do you know someone at XYZ firm?"

When you grant people permission to say no, they appreciate it, and then the next time the two of you encounter each other, it's comfortable. You've been persistent, but you haven't stalked.

Summary: Know how to ask for help, know how to say thank you, and know how to give people the opportunity to say no.

Experience Project

Armen Berjikly, creator of Experience Project

Armen Berjikly started Experience Project to help an ill friend. She was alone with her diagnosis, and friends wanted to help, yet it can be tedious for an ill person to take on the job of being a scheduler for do-gooders.

Enter Experience Project, where you can connect online with others who are in a similar situation. Most of the communication is online (rather than face-to-face). If someone isn't mobile, this is a great way to share experiences, fears, and hopes, and make connections with others who are in your situation.

The two largest communities are people who face loneliness and people with depression. At first I was a bit concerned, wishing that people would get out, make friends, and not suffer alone. But Armen reminded me that people aren't alone when they get support online and have someone who really understands them.

See www.ExperienceProject.com

13

How to Maintain and Grow Your Network

It's unlikely that you would wake up one morning and say, "I'm going to run the Boston Marathon today" without having prepared for the event. Networking is the same way. To be sure that your network is valuable to you when you need it, you need to keep it strong and healthy when you *don't* need it! When you maintain your network, you will never have to start from scratch again. Remember the effort that went into building it; now take care of it.

Here are some ideas:

- Once or twice a month, meet with someone you like—business or personal—and ask what you can do for him.
- Get involved with a professional association—get a leadership position or join a committee.
- Meet with your networking support groups (particularly your peer-to-peer team) on a regular basis—I suggest at least once a month.

- Write, speak, teach.
- Keep your personal blog or Web site up-to-date.

Create a list of "aspirational" people whose habits (and hopefully success!) you wish to emulate. We did this in a class I taught for MBAs. Warren Buffett and Bill Gates were the top two people that the students wanted to meet. After the exercise, they realized that the people they really wanted to meet were these men's assistants! Just because someone is famous or wealthy doesn't mean that you will get his attention. Join his fan club instead. If you really want to connect with him, find out who are the people he trusts and navigate toward them.

MAINTAIN YOUR NETWORK WITH PRESENT CLIENTS

In order to maximize your business contacts, you need to come up with a plan that will help you gain confidence when asking others to help you and also allow you to do some tracking of your present network. Here are some techniques.

Build your confidence by staying in regular contact with your clients, particularly those with whom you can speak candidly. The latest business term for this is "customer relationship management," but it's really just common sense. Because you like them, and we'll assume they also like you, you will get high-quality feedback. They will feel honored that you singled them out for special attention.

Here are some guidelines on why and how to network with present clients.

- Keep track of your client's expansion plans. The client may be ready to close a sale that will double its size, so that it will need more of your product or services.
- Build relationships before you need them. When a client relationship has gone sour isn't the time to invite the client to a special event in the community or a sports game.

- Consider bringing along someone else from the company who can help manage the relationship. This can be an excellent opportunity to invest in a rising star at the office by mentoring her. It's also a time when you can learn what is happening in the ranks that you may not be aware of.
- Ask the client for nothing except what you can do to help his business grow.
- Does the client have an open position and can't find the right candidate?
- Is the client less than satisfied with a service provider and seeking a new one?
- Is there a prospect that the client wants to close but can't seem to get a decision from?
- From what you've learned, come up with at least two or three things you can do that will make the client's life easier. In the course of a conversation, I once learned that someone was looking for a new team member. There were certain skill sets that the client wanted this person to have. A day or so before, I had learned of someone who had done similar work, so I made an introduction that led to a job for one and a happy employee for the other.
  - If one of the client's children has a new hobby, offer to connect the client to someone who can mentor the child.
  - Introduce the client to a new supplier.
  - Make a call to a prospect on the client's behalf.
  - Invite the client to an industry event where she can get some visibility.
  - Follow up within a week and provide an update.
- Put in a call each month to find out if there is anything new.

- The more you give, the more you get!
- Do the same for each of your other clients until the list is complete.

Remember, people are a bit like plants: They need to be watered, have good sunlight and fresh air, and on occasion be repotted. Jeff Taylor, founder of Monster.com, said, "When you are unemployed is when you deploy your network—not when you create it."[1] The same is true when you are making business development calls or requests for a nonprofit cause. Here are some thoughts:

- *Get started.* Be the one to get the relationship going. Take the initiative. Starting is often the hardest part. Make it easy for the other person. When the other person sees your energy and get-it-done attitude, he will share the information with others.
- *Create a system.* This can be index cards or a sophisticated software program. It doesn't matter; what does matter is that you use it.
- *When someone comes to mind, call her.* People like to know that they are thought of and, most important, that you took the time to connect.
- *Send thank-you notes.*
- *Send articles.* Don't assume that I've read an article that would be of interest to me. When you send me an article, it reminds me that we share an interest. And as long as you don't stalk, you add a bit of currency to our business relationship.

In *The Tipping Point*, author Malcolm Gladwell states that it is our acquaintances that grow our networks.[2] It is when we reach beyond our present community that we grow and expand into new markets.

Bob Metcalfe founded 3Com Corporation and designed the Ethernet protocol for computer networks. Metcalfe's Law states, "The usefulness, or utility, of a network equals the square of the number of users." [3]

In plain English, that means that if two people have cell phones, that's nice for them, but the technology is useless for everyone else. The more people who have phones, the more valuable the network becomes.

When two computers are networked, they can exchange information. The more computers that are networked, the more they can share. The same is true with people. Networking is an exchange. Get the wheels started and fuel the process.

> *Summary: It's much easier to network with people who you've had previous contact. Maintaining connections should be a networking priority.*

I always do what I say I'm going to do.
>   ~ FIONA WILSON, professor at Simmons College and
>   known in Boston as a "networking node"

PROFESSIONAL ASSOCIATIONS AND COMMUNITY ORGANIZATIONS

Professional associations are for people from the same industry or those who serve it. Community organizations are less targeted. It is crucial that you get involved with at least one organization at some point if you want your career to advance. This is where you can gain visibility within your industry with your peers, colleagues, competitors, vendors, and others. After you have attended several events, ask yourself:

- Have I gotten any business from the organization?
- What role (if any) do I have?
- Would it be worthwhile to join a committee?
- Is there an opportunity for me to be on a panel, be the speaker, or introduce the speaker?
- Who from my firm is the keeper of the relationship with that organization?
- Is that person the right one for the job?
- What organizations should I consider joining in the next three to six months? Why? To further my career or get business for my company?

Visit a new organization or meeting at least once a month. In doing so, consider the following:

- Determine the value of the group.
- Decide who should be the relationship manager.
- Create an action plan with next steps and a timetable.
- Find a networking partner to hold you accountable and vice versa.

Summary: It's easy to "over-join" groups. Start small and grow your participation.

PEOPLE WHO MAKE THINGS HAPPEN

Earlier in the book, I spoke about the three different types of people—those who make it happen, those who watch it happen, or those who wonder what happened. I also mentioned Benjamin Franklin and the "club for mutual improvement." I encourage you to be one of the people who make it happen. Get active!

Participate in a few carefully selected groups in areas such as investments, wine, books, sports, or others that are of interest to you.

It's easy to focus too much on our business education; do something that is completely the opposite. Learn chess, a foreign language, or a new sport. In each of these communities, you will meet new people whom you can help, and vice versa. Through online resources like Meetup.com, it is easier than ever to find or even start a group around your interests.

Things to Consider When Creating a Business-centric Networking Club

If you want to create a business-centric networking club, here are some things to consider:

- What is the membership duration?
- How often are meetings held?
- Where are they held?
- How are new members brought in?
- How are board members elected? Are there term limits?
- What is your mission statement?
- Invite business owners from different industries who are not competitors.
- How do you define a competitor? This is crucial, because sometimes we think that someone is a competitor, but upon further review find that he is not. For example, someone who works at an auditing firm will surely encounter other CPAs in his career. In some cases, they may actually end up working together. They may serve different sectors or different size companies as well.

Summary: If you see a need for a group, start one!

Invited to Join a Club?

I refuse to join any club that would have me as a member.

~ Groucho Marx

When you are invited to join any group, here are some things to consider:

- Who recommended the club?
- Are the fees and attendance requirements compatible with your lifestyle?
- Does the location lend itself to your attending?
- What are your goals, and does the club help you achieve them?
- Have you felt welcomed?
- Select only one or two groups in which to participate in the beginning, and give each at least six months.

Summary: Throughout our lives our priorities shift. Your participation in organizations will follow.

ALUMNI GROUPS

We touched on this during the inventory exercise in Chapter 3. (See the section "Inventory Your Network" and Figure 3-1.) Now that you know more, revisit this network and look for opportunities.

- Make a list of all the schools you have attended. Also list where you've worked. Alumni groups aren't just for academia.
- Ask your executive team to do the same.
- Are there alumni groups in your area?
- Do they have regular meetings?
- When was the last time you attended one?
- Is there a visible role that you can play within one of these organizations?
- Do any of them have a LinkedIn group or a Facebook page?

Summary: You have many shared experiences with these people. Reach out and make connections.

VOLUNTEERING

Volunteering is one of the best ways to grow your network. Without fail, almost every client I have I can trace back to someone I met through some volunteer effort.

When you volunteer your time, you immediately put yourself in a new category in people's eyes. You are more than just a business professional; you are someone who cares about your community and is willing to roll up your sleeves and do something extra to make a contribution. Get active in a few strategic organizations.

There are a variety of important factors to consider:

- Does this group provide services by vertical market, or does it serve a special level of attendee? (A *vertical market* is a group of similar businesses and customers that engage in trade based on specific and specialized needs.)
- Are the people who attend decision makers, or do they influence the decision makers?
- Do I like the people I meet?
- What is the required commitment of my time and other resources?
- Be sure you have time to honor your commitment; if you do not, it will come across that you were using the organization for your own personal gain and were not sincere about your offer.
- If you made a mistake, admit it, help find a replacement, and move on.

Summary: Commit only to things that you really care about and can carry out. It will hurt you in the long run if you say that you'll take something on and you don't.

HOW TO HOLD INTERNAL NETWORKING MEETINGS

Many companies have an intranet. The purpose is to streamline internal communication, which is good. Take the time saved and host face-to-face internal networking sessions. Don't feel alone if your company hasn't done this yet. This is simple to do, is very cost- and time-effective, and builds morale. Here are some guidelines:

- The purpose is to provide a forum where people can share ideas, request a solution for a problem, and take a break from work.
- To start out, schedule the meetings once a month and put them on the calendar for the next three months.
- Continue on a monthly basis, or consider holding meetings more frequently if the group would like it.
- Senior management must commit to attending and not canceling the session.
- Consider bringing in an outside facilitator. If you do not, find someone who is in middle management to facilitate— not at the top, but not too junior either.
- Test with a group of 50 or less.
- Serve soft drinks and snacks.
- The first 10 minutes should be for people to say hello to one another, get something to drink, and settle in.
- If the facilitator notices that people don't know one another, she can jump in and start making introductions happen.
- About 10 minutes into the event, the facilitator introduces herself, welcomes everyone, and states the purpose of the session.
- Suggest that one or two members of senior management say a word or two also, welcoming the group and adding

their requests—"We're looking for a new vice president of engineering" or "My daughter has a school project on frogs, so if anyone is a frog expert, please let me know."

- Have some 3" × 5" index cards and pens available on the tables. Tell the attendees that they can pick up cards and write down their name, contact information, and what they can do to solve the problem.

- Business requests can be as simple as, "I'm trying to figure out how to create a table in Microsoft Word." Or an account executive can ask if anyone knows someone at such and such company.

- The goal is to create a fun environment that is professional, but is also conducive to information exchange within the company.

- If this isn't possible in person, consider using one of the online tools such as Skype or ooVoo.

WRITING AND SPEAKING OPPORTUNITIES

Writing and speaking are two highly effective ways to increase your visibility—and therefore your network. You get instant credibility, for example, when a newspaper or magazine publishes your article. When you speak at a professional association, you get visibility and recognition from your peers that your competitors don't. Maximize these forums for your benefit.

Writing

Publications always want high-quality content written by people in the industry. This is a great way to get your name and your company's name in front of numerous people in a cost-effective manner. When you write an article, you are considered an authority. It costs soft dollars—your time—rather than cash from an advertising budget. Some of the good things about an article are that it has a long shelf life and it can be shared with others. Here are some things to consider:

1. *Select a publication that your clients read.* You want them to see you in a new venue. You can also start your own "publication" with a blog. (See the section "Personal Web Sites," in Chapter 12.) Having content that is already created and viewable will help you get a foot in the door to contribute to on- and offline publications.

2. *Comment on people's blogs.* This helps to promote your blog or Web site; hopefully the blogger will comment on your site, as well, helping to grow your network.

3. *Realize that writing is never finished.* When the deadline has arrived and the article is done, let it go! Don't be a perfectionist.

4. *Write often and write short, informative pieces.* Frequency is preferable to length.

5. *Tell a story.* Make it personal. It's easier to read and more memorable.

6. *Don't pitch your product or your company.* Your article will never see the light of day if it's a puff piece.

7. *Write with a sense of humor.* This makes an article much easier to read.

8. *Work with a public relations agency.*

9. *Write letters to the editor.*

Summary: Writing is an excellent way to gather your thoughts and share them with a wide audience without leaving the comfort of your couch.

Speaking

Are you an introvert? Then you'll make an excellent speaker! It seems counterintuitive, but what is ideal is that when you have the stage, you are completely in charge of the situation. Remember, it's *Saturday Night LIVE*, not *Saturday Night Unrehearsed*. Many speakers are introverts or tend to be shy. I know; it works for me.

I like speaking because I can lead the conversation, and when I'm comfortable and fully prepared, the interactive factor is energizing. There is a live exchange between you and the audience. This provides an opportunity for spontaneous banter. Because this aspect is not rehearsed, it is important for you to know your material and know it cold. This is not the best place to learn about your product or service and the nuances that differentiate you from your competitors. This is a preferred forum for more senior management team members who have credibility in their industry, are confident of their knowledge of the material, and have solid public speaking experience.

If you or someone in your company has this kind of opportunity or is a rising star, make the investment and hire a presentation coach. It will pay off. People will not always remember the person's name; however, they will remember the company's name. Your skills reflect not only on you, but also on your firm, industry, family, community, and more.

If you are invited to speak, here are some guidelines:

1. *Know the audience.* Weeks in advance, not the night before, find out who will be attending your presentation. If possible, find out the specific attendees so that you can read their bios.

2. *Prepare.* I find it totally insulting to hear a speaker say that the night before, he had no idea what he was going to say. (If that is the case, don't share it!) If the audience isn't that important to you, then don't agree to speak.

3. *Dress for the event.* Your dress reflects your self-image. Be appropriate, and then up it a notch out of respect for the situation.

4. *Inform, don't sell.* You have been invited because you have knowledge that is considered valuable to the listeners. If you want to sell your product, then contact an ad agency. However, your positive impact and impression will help to sell your product or brand.

5. *Get the lay of the land.* Find the room where you will be presenting and check out all the equipment a few hours before.

6. *Share an example.* Telling an anecdote makes you human and accessible. It is also much more memorable than straight fact sharing.

7. *Avoid jargon.* If you use words that are unfamiliar to the audience, you will sound pretentious and lose your listeners.

8. *Include contact information.* It's frustrating to an attendee not to know how to get in touch with you. Your coordinates should be on each page of your handouts.

9. *Turn off the cell phone.* Be sure your toys are turned off. It's quite embarrassing when the ringing phone turns out to be yours. Once I saw a speaker leave the lectern and rifle through his briefcase to turn off his phone.

10. *Use rehearsed spontaneity!* Practice! Practice! Practice! When you know your material and the audience that you are presenting to, you will be more relaxed and more interesting to listen to.

If the thought of speaking just terrifies you, take comfort. Public speaking is people's number one fear—greater than the fear of death. With practice and help, you can overcome your worries and be a fine public speaker.

For years my neck would break out in a huge red splotchy rash. I had taken speech in high school and college; however, later in life, I hit a wall of fright. Even in the summer, I would wear turtlenecks that went as high as possible. Quickly I realized that this was quite detrimental to my business, to put it mildly. I also realized that people liked the information that they learned from me and that I was cheating them if I didn't share it. But my heart would race, my breath would become short, and I just wanted to be anywhere else. Overcoming the fear was no small task.

Two things helped: breathing exercises and proper preparation. When I feel flustered these days, I back my heels to the edge of the wall, stand straight, and take long, deep breaths. One time I was asked to participate in a discussion about networking with a sales team. We discussed expectations and the forum. When I arrived, things had changed, and instead of having an interactive discussion with a few people, I was suddenly expected to deliver a presentation for 20. I immediately felt my neck flame. I stepped out, got a tall glass of water, and did some deep breathing exercises. It helped immensely.

At the root of the angst is a normal fear of failure or embarrassment. We are human; we don't want to make fools of ourselves. David Letterman said in an interview with Ted Koppel, "I have a very low threshold of embarrassment. I just don't like embarrassing myself. You know we have this—the theatre and the machinery and the people—and every day we try to put on a new show . . . and it all comes down to one hour, 5:30 to 6:30. If I somehow do something stupid that embarrasses me, I feel like I've thrown away that effort for the day. It's very frustrating. . . . I think humans just don't want to embarrass themselves."[4]

Plenty of well-known performers, such as Barbra Streisand and Carole King, have experienced stage fright and thus imprisoned themselves in a recording studio. Through courage and friendship, they mustered the guts to take the stage again until they learned to conquer their fears.

We all want to be accepted and appreciated, and the thought of failure or humiliation is real. The truth is that practice improves our skills. If we practice avoidance, we will perfect our fear. By taking on the challenge and facing our worries, we put fear behind us and do not cheat others of our knowledge.

Start—just start. Begin speaking to small groups and run a few meetings—the more you do it, the less fearful you will be. Don't rob others of your knowledge. Do it for you!

Summary: Speaking is an effective and efficient way to share your knowledge and meet many people.

I cannot give you the formula for success, but I can give you the formula for failure—try to please everybody.
~ HERBERT BAYARD SWOPE

JOINING BOARDS

The act of self-giving is a personal power-releasing factor.
~ NORMAN VINCENT PEALE

Serving on a board, either corporate or nonprofit, is an excellent way to make connections with people that you otherwise would not meet. Those who are unfamiliar with board duties may hesitate to commit to a board, especially after debacles such as Enron or Tyco. There are typically two types of boards for most companies: the board of advisors and the board of directors. The former is responsible for advice; the latter is responsible for both advice and financial management of the organization.

Start with an advisory position. Get to know the players in the community, and determine whether the position suits you personally and professionally. Board responsibilities can take a lot of time, and it's important to review the net results of any business or company awareness that comes from your role.

Nonprofit boards offer a different opportunity and a good introduction to board management. Ask around, find an organization that is compatible with your values, and find a way to serve. Start with a short term—one year. Nonprofits will expect you to make a cash donation and to help with fund-raising. Find out what is expected of you before you sign up.

CAUSE-RELATED NETWORKING

Whether you pick a cause for personal or business reasons, it will reflect on both. Ask yourself why this organization appeals to you and whether this is the best use of your time. If the purpose is to grow your business, will this interfere with your business development efforts or enhance them? Be sure the audience meets the same criteria you have for a new customer.

- About 76 percent of consumers report that they would be likely to switch to a brand associated with a good cause (Cone/Roper Report, 2007).
- About 90 percent of workers whose companies have a cause program feel proud of their companies' values (Cone/Roper Report, 2009).

Here are some examples of cause-related programs:

- McDonald's and Conservation International
- Timberland and City Year
- MBNA and Ducks Unlimited
- Johnson & Johnson and Save the Children

One of the fastest-growing ways for companies to create visibility is to participate in a cause-related marketing campaign. "Cause-related marketing [CRM] refers to a commercial activity in which companies and nonprofit organizations form alliances to market an image, product or service for mutual benefit,"[5] according to the Business for Social Responsibility organization. Remarkably enough, CRM also stands for customer relationship management. The two are interrelated in terms of the way you manage and leverage the assets of both groups.

Targeting Women Entrepreneurs

Gail Snowden and Amy Geogan of Bank Boston, charter sponsors of the Center for Women and Enterprise in Boston

Gail Snowden and Amy Geogan at Bank Boston saw an opportunity. Small loans to women business owners had a strong repayment track record and were highly profitable. They came up with what they thought was a brilliant business idea: target women entrepreneurs.

The two made their business case to the bank executives and suggested that the bank sponsor a new nonprofit targeting women entrepreneurs. The bank was unconvinced, so the two found $50,000 out of their operating budgets to be the charter sponsors of the Center for Women and Enterprise in Boston. Soon the female entrepreneur was one of the fastest-growing and attractive markets in banking, and Bank Boston was at the forefront.

During this process, Gail and Amy developed a strong network that gave them visibility in the Boston area and the growing entrepreneur network. While serving on the board, they made contacts that they otherwise would not have made. As more companies looked for working and expansion capital, the phone and profits started ringing at Bank Boston. The program was so successful that the bank decided to support other organizations serving the women's business community.

Neither of these women was the top executive of the company. They had budgetary responsibility, and they saw this as a business opportunity. The program's success gave the bank as well as those championing it visibility in the community.

Here are some key things to remember:

- Take care of your business and your personal reputation.
- Treat the organization as if it were a paying client. Be on time with reports and deliverables.
- Underpromise and overdeliver.

While strategic partnerships with nonprofits can be very beneficial, they can also take time and energy. It is important for you to conduct the same due diligence that you would with a for-profit partner. Nonprofits are typically short on resources—both people and money. Be clear about what you are able to provide (and expect), as well as what you cannot do.

When I worked for a nonprofit, we created several partnerships. One was with a cruise line, and another was with a manufacturing company. The cruise partnership was to provide funds for research. Through my former travel network, I learned that the company had recently been fined for environmental violations. In addition, the grant money came from casino profits. Now the nonprofit was taking "dirty" money.

The manufacturing company made its product in the third world and used child labor. It abided by the laws of the local country; however, some of the staff at the nonprofit were less than convinced that this partnership was a good idea. The company was looking to leverage the visibility of the nonprofit to enter a new market and show its product in action. Management team members for both organizations changed, and the new players didn't develop the same rapport.

Both deals worked for a while, but they didn't survive in the long run. There wasn't enough of a bond and commitment by both parties.

Before you invest your company dollars and energy, here are some questions to ask when considering a partnership:

- Are the mission and values of the two organizations aligned?

- Who is on each board?
- Is the nonprofit a 501(c)(3)? (This is important for tax reasons.)
- Have the management teams met?
- Has either organization done this type of partnership before?
- Who is the relationship manager from each side?
- What resources will be allocated to the partnership?

OTHER NETWORKING FORUMS

A network is made up of a group of people who share an interest. A unique bond exists. In order to participate and feel comfortable, everyone needs to speak the same language, if you will. Here are some examples:

- George went to work one day and had no idea what people were talking about. Apparently he was the only one who had not seen *Seinfeld* the night before. In order to participate in the office conversations, he started watching the show. He intentionally changed his behavior in order to fit in.
- I started a seminar called "Water Cooler Football." The idea was to help people understand the conversation around the water cooler about a football game. The attendees were nonathletic men, women, and non-U.S. nationals. The story made it into *Newsweek*. See www.EffectiveNetworking.com and click on Press.
- When you walk by an office building, there is a networking group right outside—the smokers. They understand one another's needs in a way that nonsmokers don't. (*Note:* This is *not* a recommendation that you start smoking!)

- HOG[6] is a community that is 650,000 strong. What do they have in common? They own Harley-Davidson motorcycles—Harley Owners Group.

- A strong and successful community is the 12-step recovery model. There is an understanding of a life challenge that others may not understand or appreciate. These groups are designed to provide a forum where people can share their fears and aspirations. The mission is not to get business, but the currency exchanged is often much more valuable than money. The anonymity is essential to provide a safe place for conversation. More and more "meetings" are held online or by phone.

- In parent-to-be groups, everyone is filled with anticipation and great joy. At the same time, each person realizes that her life is about to change dramatically. This also applies to weight-loss groups.

- When a member of our family becomes ill, we often feel alone. Learning that someone else is experiencing the same pain can help ease the burden and emptiness. Online support groups have mushroomed in the past few years.

- Fraternities and sororities are other examples of networking forums. When you see someone in an airport with a sweatshirt with the name of your house, you immediately sense a connection. A conversation can be readily started.

Summary: There are many groups out there—find one where you can learn, contribute, and be successful.

Building an Online Social Network

Roger Glovsky, founding partner, Indigo Venture Law Offices

Roger Glovsky is a founding partner of Indigo Venture Law Offices, a business law firm based in Massachusetts that provides legal counsel to entrepreneurs and high-tech businesses. Mr. Glovsky is also founder of LEXpertise.com, a collaboration and networking site for lawyers, and writes blogs for iLaw2.com, The Virtual Lawyer, and askthevc.com. I asked him to discuss how social networking sites could potentially factor into one's professional development:

One way to use social networking Web sites is to build your own. Five years ago, John Koenig and I started the Business Lawyers Network (www.businesslawyersnet.com), which is a group of about 400 independent lawyers and other professionals. John and I each started with our own Rolodex, which was built serendipitously over time. I knew three patent lawyers, but no estate planning attorneys. He knew estate planning lawyers, but no criminal lawyers. As business lawyers, we wanted to strengthen and expand our network, both for referral purposes and to have access to certain legal skills that our clients might need in the future.

We started the BLN by meeting in person and sending meeting announcements using a simple e-mail list. At the meeting, we handed out attendance lists with the names of all participants. Quickly, the maintenance of a contact database, sending our announcements, and preparing contact lists became time-consuming and tedious. About two years ago, we moved the group to a social networking Web site that was built using Drupal, a free open-source Web application. The advantage of having a social networking Web site is that members keep their own profiles and contact information up-to-date. The members use the Web site to sign up for events, and the system automatically sends out notices (and reminders) of the upcoming meetings. This greatly facilitated the growth and effectiveness of the network.

Moving the group from offline to online was initially a challenge. First, lawyers are generally reluctant to use technology. I like to say that lawyers embrace "trailing-edge" technology; they are usually the last ones to incorporate technological change into their profession. Second, our members were reluctant to join a previously unknown Web site, which we called LEXpertise (www.LEXpertise.

com). They were just beginning to sign up for well-known Web sites like LinkedIn and Facebook and weren't even sure whether they wanted to participate in those Web sites.

So, how did we did we get our members online? The simple answer is that we did not give them a choice.

The primary reason that members came to our events was for networking purposes. They wanted to meet lawyers and other professionals who could refer business to them and whom they might want to refer business to. They needed to meet in person because lawyers play the role of trusted advisors. Lawyers cannot refer business to people that they don't know personally. A bad referral would adversely affect the lawyer's trust relationship with his client. If the client asks, "How do you know this person?" the lawyer does not want to say that she met the person online. What she does want to say is that she knows him personally and has gotten to know him over some period of time.

The attendance list, which we handed out at every meeting, showed the name and contact information for each participant. That way, several months later, when a referral opportunity arose, the lawyer could remember whom she had met at the BLN event and how to contact him. The attendance list was the critical piece for getting lawyers to join our Web site. In order for their names and contact information to appear on the attendance list, lawyers had to first sign up for the event online. In order to sign up for the event online, the lawyers had to create an online account and fill out a profile. And only those who created an online account and filled out the profile would have their names and contact information appear on the attendance list.

One question you might ask is why we did not use an existing social networking site such as LinkedIn or Facebook. That is because those sites are too large and are inconsistent with creating a smaller trusted community of referral sources. Also, by building our own Web site, we have more control over the features and services that we can offer to the network as it grows.

The bottom line is that we gave our members a reason why they had to sign up on our social networking Web site. After the members joined our Web site, the BLN group and the events were much easier to manage and much easier to grow.

14

Ethics

A lie has speed, but truth has endurance.

~ EDGAR J. MOHN

Always do right. This will gratify some people and astonish the rest.

~ MARK TWAIN

In recent times, business scandals have led to a renewed interest in ethics. As with almost anything, there is a fine line, and sometimes that line isn't clear until it has been crossed. Networking is no different. As I interviewed various successful professionals, I heard stories of people misrepresenting whom they know, their accomplishments, and even where they received their education.

Notre Dame and Dartmouth found themselves in the embarrassing situation of having to dismiss a new hire before the person even started. The U.S. Olympic Committee learned that its chair really didn't have a doctorate, as she had stated on her résumé.[1]

Your reputation is your most valuable life asset, both professionally and personally. Take pride in what you do, give proper credit to those who have been a part of your success, and always be honest.

You will never regret it. It's easy to imagine that the team at Enron would like to redo a number of the decisions it made that proved catastrophic for the individuals involved and many others.

Being ethical isn't the property of one gender, race, culture, or any other defined group. It's a behavior choice. When you are networking, state the facts. These guidelines are relevant both online and offline. Here are some ways to protect yourself:

- Use someone's name only when you have been given permission to do so.
- Preferably ask someone to do an e-intro and/or make a call introducing you.
- It's okay to say, "I met John Jones at a trade show last week, and he mentioned your name. I doubt that he would remember me, since he certainly met a lot of people that day."
- When in doubt, underplay your connection to the other person.
- You do not want to lead the other person to believe that you have been endorsed. If you are being endorsed or recommended, a letter or e-mail of introduction is appropriate.

Here's what I say when I write an e-intro. Conservatively, I write several a week:

Roberta and Michelle—this is an e-intro from Diane Darling. The two of you should meet, and here are my thoughts.

Michelle works for a company that is looking to donate a marketing tool to a nonprofit.

Roberta is the executive director of a nonprofit that would value your services.

Here is the contact information for both. (Include e-mail addresses and phone numbers.)

(I used to say, "Over to the two of you!" and then I realized that neither person would act, since neither of them knew who should start the dialogue. So now I "assign" it to the person that I know is most eager to get the conversation started.)

If you have any questions, please don't hesitate to contact me.

Best—Diane

When you access someone under false pretenses, in due time it will be discovered. Don't risk it.

Here are some good guidelines for workplace ethics from *Power Etiquette*[2]:

- Don't participate in gossip.
- Be courteous and respectful to superiors and subordinates.
- Be positive and pleasant.
- Accept constructive criticism.
- Maintain your personal dignity.
- Make an effort to preserve the dignity of others.
- Keep confidences and maintain confidentiality.
- Show your concern for others.
- Give credit to those who deserve it.
- Be honest.
- Keep your word.
- Encourage and help others to do their best.
- Make practical and constructive suggestions for improvement.

On occasion, you may want to confide in someone that you are starting a business or job hunting. Be cautious about the situation you are putting this person in. Are you compromising her job or relationships at all?

Unless we tell people what our ethical boundaries are, we cannot assume that both people see the same situation through the same glasses. In fact, if you are increasingly feeling imposed upon, it is probable that your expectations are indeed different. At that point, you can choose to either say something or back away. It depends on the value of the relationship.

As you think about networking, here are some ethical guidelines to consider in three key areas of professional life: making calls, providing references, and writing a résumé.

MAKING CALLS

It's intimidating to call people we don't know, even if someone has given us an introduction. Sometimes people use a variety of techniques to get access to someone. In some cases it's genuine; however, there are times when it is less than honest.

1. Have permission before using someone's name. Imagine that she is witnessing the conversation with you.
2. Respect the limits of your relationship. Don't overstate how well you know someone. The world is very small (and becoming increasingly so).
3. Be thoughtful of someone's time. Keep the call on topic and to the point.
4. Thank the person for his time and ideas.
5. Write a thank-you note, or at least send an e-mail. I suggest that you do both—you look both prompt and classy!

BUSINESS OR PERSONAL REFERENCES

Frankly, I pay little attention to references. I assume that the ones I'm being given are happy clients or contented former employers. This is where networking is either your friend or your foe. Any business community or industry is just a small community, when you get right down to it. Ask around and get the story behind the story.

If you have people in your past who, when asked, will say less than flattering things about you, address the issue quickly. Be proactive. In many cases there were two different styles or perspectives, and it was best for both parties to move forward separately.

I had a consultant, we'll call her Mary, who approached me with some ideas that were interesting, but I was cautious about working with her. It was really just a gut feeling. She gave me references, but I recalled a few people she mentioned that she had worked for. One afternoon, when I had a few minutes, I called several of them and left messages. I knew Maxine, so it was an opportunity for me to reconnect with her as well.

The following day I got a call from Mary saying that she had heard that I was checking references with Maxine. Mary then went on to explain that Maxine rarely returns calls, so it was unlikely that I would hear from her.

Hmm—if Maxine doesn't return calls, why did she return Mary's and not mine? It left me suspicious of Mary's work.

RÉSUMÉS

Your résumé should be both complete and accurate. Find someone who specializes in writing them. It will be worth your effort, time, and investment. If you think it is expensive, consider the alternative.

Summary: If you have to ask yourself if something is right or wrong, you already have the answer. Your career spans your life, not just one or two jobs. Be sure that your behavior reflects your values (and those of the people who love you).

15

What If I Don't Feel Like Networking?

First of all, remind yourself what networking really is. It is *not* transactional; it is relational. If you are in need of a client, an employee, a job, or a charity donation, then be realistic—you are not really networking. You have a task at hand, and you need to complete it.

Ask yourself why you don't want to go to an event, or why you don't want to make the call. What is the *real* reason that you don't want to attend? In some cases, it's simply that you are tired and have been working extra hours, or that the location of the event is not that convenient to your office. The location and logistics of getting to a destination play an important role in your decision. That's fine.

Note: The word *event* could mean a conference, meeting, trade show, dinner party, cocktail reception, luncheon meeting—any type of interaction with others that will require your participation.

What you want to avoid is not attending an event for other reasons, such as fear of talking to people, intimidation, or concern that you won't fit in.

Practice makes perfect. If you practice not attending, then you will become an expert on *not* going to networking events. Do you honestly want to be highly skilled at missing opportunities to meet future clients, friends, vendors, or employees?

As stated earlier, online networking continues to grow in popularity and acceptance. I sometimes get e-mails from people ahead of time who are attending a conference or event. Some ask a question in advance, and others say welcome. When I speak on a panel, I try to e-mail the other guests and introduce myself.

HOW TO PSYCH YOURSELF UP

Sometimes going is not optional—we must attend an event. When that is the case, it's all up to you (and your attitude) how the event will turn out.

Here are some ideas that may make it easier:

- Arrive on the early side. Personally, I find it easier to walk into a quieter room than into one that is full of cliques.
- Unless you are the guest of honor, the event isn't really about you. I encourage you to focus your thinking on what you can do for others in the room rather than on what you can get. This helps take away the pressure.
- Find a networking buddy to attend the function with you.
- Treat yourself to a cab rather than public transportation and arrive in a peaceful state of mind.
- Research the event's Web site for 15 minutes and write out your neutral questions.
- Remember a positive experience you had once before when you didn't "feel" like going.
- Consider the experience a "practice" event.
- Try a new introduction or challenge yourself to walk up to a few people and introduce yourself even when you really don't want to.

- Find one or two jokes that you can confidently tell. Practice them on a total stranger.
- Wear something that makes you feel great.

In many cases, you'll find that it isn't as bad as you expected. In fact, frequently within 10 to 20 minutes, you find yourself in a great conversation that you otherwise would not have experienced.

Most people I've met consider networking something that needs to be done, not something that they want to do. When the discussion goes a bit deeper, it turns out that because networking is considered an important skill, there is an expectation that we know what to do. In reality, we haven't taken any courses in it, so it's a trial by fire experience.

Since networking doesn't immediately provide something tangible, we tend to discount its value and thus avoid it. When we practice avoidance, we lose our networking know-how, and that leads to discomfort.

Summary: If you don't feel like networking, think with the end in mind. If you knew how the conversation or event would end, would you feel hesitant?

WE DON'T KNOW WHAT TO SAY

This is one of the most frequent comments I hear. We put so much pressure on ourselves to say something that's meaningful or memorable. We forget that we can start with, "Hello, how are you?"

Joe was an accomplished young law associate. He was starting out in his law career, and he didn't see himself as someone who could bring in business for his firm or make an impact on the bottom line. He happened to be in Boston and came in for one of our workshops. A few days later, he was at the garage dropping off his car to be repaired and getting a cab back to his office. The person next to him suggested that they share a cab.

During the training session, we had discussed conversation openers. Not sure of what to say during the ride, he started the conversation by talking about the fun dogs in the park as the cab drove into the city. After a few exchanges, they began to talk about what they did. It turned out that she was the general counsel for a company that his firm had been trying to approach.

Summary: It's worth it to be friendly. You never know!

WE FEEL LIKE WE'RE BOTHERING PEOPLE

We're bothering people only if we don't know what we want or what we have to offer. In that case, we are not thinking about others; we just are thinking about ourselves. Shift the focus to the other person. Each day people ask for help. Sometimes it's small—what supplier do you use for your business cards? Sometimes it's big—we're looking for $10 million in venture capital to start a technology business.

Most people would like to help people, preferably with the least hassle to themselves. If they know what your product or service is, or that you are seeking a new job, they can help everyone involved.

Summary: With all due respect, if you are thinking about yourself, it's harder to help others. Frame your request in a way that it matters to other person. It's fine if you succeed as well.

WE DON'T WANT TO APPEAR NEEDY

Neither does the other person. This is a hopeless standoff—someone has to speak first. When you have done your preparation and your analysis of why you are networking and with whom, then you will be genuine and sincere. You will know what you have to offer and what the other person may need.

Having a need is very different from being needy. A need can typically be solved quickly and with one action—the right hire, funding for the business, getting a new job. Being needy is an ongoing and often draining experience for both parties. Articulate your needs.

Summary: We don't know what others need until we converse with them.

FEAR

Fear is that little darkroom where negatives are developed.
~ MICHAEL PRITCHARD

Fear can be a good thing. It stops us from doing something unwise like repeatedly arriving at work late, cheating on an exam, or being unkind to people. Walking into a room, especially one that is filled with strangers, can be absolutely terrifying. There is one simple solution to this problem: blame our parents! When we were younger and headed out the door, they were the ones who said, "Don't talk to strangers!"

The situation obviously has changed. We are no longer kids. We are adults, yet we still have childlike fears.

Here is a new look at the word *fear*:

- **F** — False
- **E** — Evidence
- **A** — Appearing
- **R** — Real

What real evidence do you have that you should be afraid of saying hello to someone at a business or social event? The answer is simple: there isn't any!

As an adult, you have gained wisdom. You know that this individual may solve a problem that you have, and vice versa. Smile, reach out your hand, and say hello. If it turns out that there isn't any reason for the two of you to continue the dialogue, wish each other well. Simply say, "It was very nice to meet you! Best of luck."

Watch children—they are fearless. We have had the childlike curiosity trained out of us. Get it back! Take a look around the room; is there really a reason for you to be intimidated by someone else who is there? It's likely that you all have something in common or you wouldn't be in the same room.

A forced conversation can feel like a nightmare. The next time we find ourselves in such a situation, we begin to worry and feel anxious. This means one thing—we are human. We want to be appreciated by others, and if we are rejected, it doesn't feel good. Therefore we ask ourselves, why risk it?

Fear of embarrassment, humiliation, rejection, shame, and all those other emotions makes us decide not to do something. Most of us did something as a kid that people made fun of. We learned from that experience not to do it again. We wanted to be accepted by our peers, and we learned what rejection felt like.

That moment also taught us that maybe we shouldn't try things that we don't know how to do. We thus shy away from unknown conversations or events to protect our self-esteem.

When you see someone with his arms crossed, that person is literally protecting his heart. In many cases, during that conversation, the person is fearful of being hurt. Past experiences have taught him that there is reason to be afraid.

Suzanne Bates is an award-winning news anchor who now teaches public speaking. We were on a panel together at a conference, and she asked one of the participants to tell her story. The woman came up to the front of the room, leaned against the table, and crossed her arms. As Suzanne asked her questions, the woman's posture began to shift. Her shoulders began to look less like her earrings. Next, she dropped her arms and put her hands on the table. Within a matter of seconds, Suzanne made this person feel cared for and important. The woman no longer felt that she needed to protect her heart by guarding it with her arms.

I have a collection of quotes on fear. Here are just a few:

- If you're never scared or embarrassed or hurt, it means you never take any chances. ~ JULIA SOREL

- Anything I've ever done that ultimately was worthwhile . . . initially scared me to death. ~ BETTY BENDER

- Do the thing you fear to do and keep on doing it. That is the quickest and surest way ever yet discovered to conquer fear. ~ DALE CARNEGIE

- Winners are those people who make a habit of doing the things losers are uncomfortable doing. ~ ED FOREMAN

- Fear defeats more people than any other one thing in the world. ~ RALPH WALDO EMERSON

- Fear of success can also be tied into the idea that success means someone else's loss. Some people are unconsciously guilty because they believe their victories are coming at the expense of another. ~ JOAN C. HARVEY

- Feel the fear and do it anyway. ~ SUSAN JEFFERS

- A champion is afraid of losing. Everyone else is afraid of winning. ~ BILLIE JEAN KING

- Fear makes strangers of people who should be friends. ~ SHIRLEY MACLAINE

- Whenever we are afraid, it's because we don't know enough. If we understood enough, we would never be afraid. ~ EARL NIGHTINGALE

Summary: Focus on the other person and your fear will begin to dissipate.

DEALING WITH NERVES

When fear does strike us—and we are all human, so it will—here are a few exercises that take away the edge and reduce the stress. These take less than two to three minutes and work wonders.[1]

Exercise 1: Tension

- In your car or your desk chair, sit where you can stretch your legs straight forward.
- Close your eyes if possible.
- Tense up your arms, legs, and shoulders and hold for 10 seconds.
- Relax.
- Take a deep breath.
- Tense up again for 10 seconds.
- Turn your head to either side, pull it down gently, and stretch your neck.
- Tense again. This time, be sure you point your heels to the ground and then point your toes forward.
- Relax your muscles. You're done in less than a minute!

Exercise 2: Breathing

- This one works well any time you are feeling the slightest bit of stress or strain. You can do this in an elevator, while walking, in your car (not necessarily when you're driving mind you!).
- Sit up straight or stand.
- Close your eyes if possible (definitely not while driving).
- Put your hands to your sides.
- Take a deep breath in to the s-l-o-w count of 4.
- Hold for four seconds.

- S-l-o-w-l-y breathe out for four seconds.
- Do this three times.
- If you are in a networking meeting or on a call and feeling anxious, this can be done anytime. It's quiet and unnoticeable.

Summary: When we are feeling tense and stressed is often when we get nervous and rush our words. In some cases, we come across as lacking confidence. In other cases, we come across as angry. Why risk a negative response? Take a breath and slow down.

WILL WE FIT IN?

This is a genuine concern from a practical standpoint as well as from an emotional one. We don't want to go to an event where we are not welcome or where we feel uncomfortable. We also want to be sure that this is the right audience for us. One of the best ways to get an answer to whether the organization might be a match for you is to ask someone who is familiar with the person or the hosting organization. What was this person's perception of the person or the group? What type of person is part of her network?

You will feel more confident if you do some pre-event preparation. Invest 5 to 15 minutes to determine whether the event passes or fails the screen test. Next, you will want to dig a bit deeper and learn more. What is your contact's role in the organization, how long has he been involved, to what other groups does he belong, and so on.

At this point, you have done more preparation work than most attendees will have even thought of.

From all that you have learned, draft several neutral questions that you can ask anyone in the room. (See the section "Conversation Starters," in Chapter 7, for some examples.)

Practice the questions out loud. Do this two or three times. Like magic, you'll feel much better, and you'll sound that way as well.

Summary: If we were teased as a kid, it's hard to erase those memories. You are now a grown up and can take charge. It's up to you.

I'M NOT SURE IT'S WORTH MY TIME AND EFFORT

Time is precious. We can't get it back, and therefore we need to invest it wisely. There isn't anything worse than finding yourself trapped at an event or in a conversation when you could be working or off enjoying yourself elsewhere. Many networking events take place before or after working hours, so it is even more important to evaluate them for their immediate and long-term value.

Preparation is the solution. Review the event "Whether Report" and determine whether or not you should attend. (See Figure 4-3 on page 81.) Now you have your answer.

ARE YOU HESITANT TO DEPLOY YOUR NETWORK?

It's great that we have a collection of wonderful people that we can help. However, we often don't call on them when we need to. We trick ourselves into believing that if they could help us, they would have done so already. Or are they too busy? Do they even know what we need? I've seen this happen to the best of networkers. It's a subtle form of self-sabotage.

People don't want to feel that they "owe" you. The best way to keep the relationship going strong is to ask them for their advice or for help in something. They will feel honored that you—a champion networker—asked them. Many of us are perfectly willing to call on our business network, but it's harder to call on our personal one. Don't interrupt the networking process. If you don't ask for help, others will be hesitant to ask when they need help. This is a full-circle effort. It's time to punt!

Begin by asking for little things. Request something that is easy for the person to say yes or no to. For example, if you ask to borrow someone's jacket to run an errand when it's cold outside, the person is likely to say yes. Of course, the person may say no because she is also heading out in a few minutes and will need it. This isn't a rejection of you; it's a turndown of that specific request.

In *Men Are from Mars, Women Are from Venus*, John Gray explains why men don't like the word *can*. Can you take out the trash? Of course they can—whether they *will* is a different question. Learn how people like to be asked to help you. It's as simple as do they speak French, German, Spanish, or English. You need to ask in the right language.

Summary: If you knew someone needed help and you had an answer, wouldn't you want to step up. The same is true for how people feel about you.

HINTING

While we may think our friends or business associates are brilliant, they really can't read our minds. Don't make it difficult. Come straight out and ask them if they know someone who would help with such and such a project.

Candidly, I find women hint way too much. Here's an example, "honey, the trash is getting a bit full." Some people are more intuitive than others. Some are just too busy in their own mind.

In many cases, people aren't sure we want their help. They are waiting for your permission. They may have offered to help in the past, and someone didn't like it. So they are concerned about offending you. Teach them that you are different and that you would very much like their assistance.

Genuinely flatter them! "Of all the people I could ask, I knew you would have the answer."

Remember the story of the person in Texas who asked for the gold bag for a black tie event on Saturday night. Make your request memorable, repeatable, and simple.

Summary: If you are not getting the help you need, try a more straightforward approach, ask.

I'M NOT THE NETWORKING TYPE—I'M SHY!

Most people think that good networkers are sociable types—outgoing, eager, people who can walk up to anyone with ease. Some of those people are indeed excellent networkers, but not necessarily.

Shy people can be excellent networkers. Networking isn't about walking into a room and slapping people on the back. It's about being genuine and sincerely interested in others. Quiet and introverted people can be very genuine and sincere. In fact, many would argue that it is the quieter people who fly under the radar who know what's really happening and who the players are.

Susan is someone I've known for nearly 10 years. We met at a slide show that a friend was giving, a book signing about his brother, who had decided to work in the circus as a clown. Needless to say, there were a variety of conversation topics at this gathering. In the years I've known Susan, I've observed that her ability to stay connected with people, sincerely care about them, make introductions, and much more, is truly an art.

Curiosity and genuine interest—these characteristics are essential to networking success.

As I researched this book, I became fascinated by the impact of shyness on people's lives. The research also helped me understand myself. While I am touted as a superb networker, that doesn't mean that I don't feel nervous when I walk up to strangers and start a conversation. As with flossing, I'm very competent at it. But I would always prefer someone to introduce herself to me rather than my making the effort.

When I surveyed a group of senior executives prior to an event, more than 60 percent said that they were either somewhat shy or very shy.

Shyness is rooted in a range of legitimate fears, namely, fear of

- Failure
- Embarrassment
- Rejection
- Humiliation
- Shame

We remember those times when we were children and someone made fun of us. If we were not in an environment where we could repeat the behavior and get a positive rather than a negative response, we assumed that we had done something wrong or bad. The next time we were in a situation where we could try the behavior again, we opted to avoid the potential embarrassment and not participate. We practiced avoidance and therefore perfected it.

As we contemplate attending an event, we can find ourselves experiencing "anticipatory anxiety." We begin to experience nervousness just thinking about it.

Vijai P. Sharma, author of *People-Fear, A Self-Help Book for Social Anxiety and Social Phobia*, says, "Social anxiety refers to the nervousness we feel when we are around people. 'Stage fright' is the nervousness or fear a performer experiences about his or her public appearance. But what is a 'stage' anyhow?"

All the world's a stage,
And all the men and women merely players.
They have their exits and their entrances;
And one man in his time plays many parts.

~ SHAKESPEARE, *As You Like It*

Nine out of ten people have stage fright.[2] For some, just introducing themselves makes them feel as if they are on stage.

Dr. Sharma reminds us of Bashful in *Snow White*, the shy and nervous character named Piglet in *Winnie-the-Pooh*, and the Lion in *The Wizard of Oz*, who is "afraid of everything and everybody."[3]

When we were children, these stories were used as a part of our character education. The Lion believes that the Wizard has the power to give him courage, only to realize that he had it all along.

Summary: Shy people may not be obvious, but they are curious and helpful.

INNER CRITIC

Not only do we have many external messages about why we should be less than thrilled to venture out, but we have internal messages as well. We hear over and over again in our minds that we should be hesitant to venture out. We hear all the reasons why we might fail. We may not fit into the group. Others know more about what they are doing than we do. Our clothes aren't right. Even our hair affects our state of mind.

With all that negativity, no wonder we are less than excited about venturing into the unknown. The truth is, we have mixed feelings. We want to attend so that we can make a contribution, share our knowledge, and help others. We also want to be accepted and appreciated. On the other hand, we could experience negative emotions—we may not be welcomed, we will feel alone if we don't find someone to talk to—and this translates into our feeling rejected.

We all have an inner critic. Networking is a perfect time to convert that voice to a positive one.

Instead of saying:

- I don't want to go. I won't meet anyone whom I can do business with. Plus, I'd rather be home watching TV.

Replace it with:

- I'll give it 15 minutes. If I don't feel inspired by then, I'll give myself permission to leave.

Instead of saying:

- The last time I went to one of these things, I just met competitors.

Replace it with:

- Competitors can be interesting to talk to. It's interesting to learn what is going on in my field.

Instead of saying:

- I don't like small talk, and I never will.

Replace it with:

- I'm going to write out three questions that I can ask anyone in the room and test them to see which one works best.

Summary: Stop being mean to yourself.

DEFINITION OF INSANITY

Many of you are familiar with the definition of insanity: doing the same thing over and over again, but expecting different results.[4] If networking is truly working for you now, change nothing. If you keep doing the same thing over and over again, but you expect a different result, maybe you should rethink your efforts.

Summary: There are endless reasons not to network. Think of the result you want and start there.

16

Gender, Race, Culture, and Other Networking Factors

Stereotypes abound. It's a fact. No matter how much we don't want to admit it, when we meet someone, we immediately bring with us a flood of stereotypes concerning the way that person should behave. Gender, race, culture, religion, age, political affiliation—whatever group we are a part of, either by birth or by choice, others have preconceived expectations of how we will behave and will approach us with that in mind. Movies and books either celebrate the differences or try to explain them.

GENDER

The two main categories we are lumped into are male and female. This starts at birth and goes on for life. The moment we walk in the door, there are assumptions made about us. This inescapably affects networking—where we network, the time we have available, and what is expected and/or permitted.

The increasing number of organizations dedicated to women in business indicates that women have not felt welcomed by men and feel a need to self-segregate. Some of this is positive and some of this can be self-defeating.

Ask not only who your clients are but who pays for your services and gives you referrals. In many cases, it's both men and women.

THE OLD BOYS' NETWORK

One of the most talked about networks is the "old boys' network." Men have been networking for a longer time than women. It's just a fact of the business world. They have had more practice and experience at it. However, this is changing as more women are in the business world and have been for a while.

The "old boys' network" exists, but it is increasingly a coed world as capable women rise through the ranks and run giant corporations. It is important for women to meet and work with men who are "in the know" and who want to facilitate introductions for talented women in the business community. Women who speak their business language and help facilitate the growth of companies will find it easier to break into the old boys' network.

Smart men are also realizing that the old boys' network isn't something that they can count on. According to the *New York Times*, 78 percent of the people who lost their jobs in this recent recession were men. It's important to have a diversified network.[1]

In June 2002, Anita Hill wrote an article for the *New York Times*[2] pointing out that the whistleblowers at Enron and the FBI were both women. *Time* chose them as Persons of the Year. Are women more ethical, or are they left out of the old boys' network and therefore feel more free to speak up? It's an interesting question, and one that doesn't have an easy answer. The bottom line of business is profit. If you can help a company grow its profits—ethically—you will be in a network of talented people of both genders.

Summary: In general men have been networking longer than women and teaching their sons how to do it. It can be awkward for both to expand but in the end it will be better for everyone to have a full network.

RACE, CULTURE, WEIGHT, AND OTHER NETWORKING FACTORS

The same is true with race and culture. Increasingly I'm being invited to speak to groups such as the Latino Professional Network or the National Association of Black MBAs. I was once invited to a conference about race and the person said, "after all white is a color too!"

There is a self-selective segregation going on so that people can reach out to like-minded others to learn, network, and do business. These organizations are growing in size and power as their members reach higher roles in companies. Companies such as Gillette and Verizon have diversity initiatives so that the company's employee base reflects its customer base.

As a child and a teen, I lived in Asia. We didn't have a TV, and neither e-mail nor the Web was used by the public. Being a racial minority was something that I learned about early. There were traits that I learned to attribute to the Thai population. Some of them were refreshing and infectious, as Thailand is indeed the "Land of Smiles."

When our family returned to the United States, we moved to Alabama. One of my most indelible memories is of the time our family went to Tuskegee Institute for the Christmas concert. There were *maybe* 10 Caucasians in the entire concert hall. As I watched the various groups head to the stage, I marveled at the casualness of the performance and the performers. There were outbursts of laughter, spontaneous applause, and audience participation. That certainly wasn't how I had been taught to behave at a religious or holiday event.

Whether they are based on race, gender, religion, or culture, we all make judgments throughout the day. Some of the popular TV shows that attempt to look at human interactions from an outsider's perspective, such as *Mork and Mindy* or *Third Rock from the Sun*, make us realize how ridiculous those assumptions are. But they are real, and it is wise for us to accept this and learn the best way to manage the situation, no matter where we are.

The film *Shallow Hal*, starring Gwyneth Paltrow, addressed the topic of weight and how we think about it.[3] Ms. Paltrow was startled at how she was treated when she was in New York wearing her "fat suit." She said, "I walked through the lobby. . . . No one would make eye contact with me because I was obese. The clothes they make for women that are overweight are horrible. I felt humiliated because people were so dismissive."

We make instant decisions about people based on these and other factors. There is nothing we can do to change this. However, smart networkers are aware of it and recognize how it can positively or negatively affect others as well as themselves.

THREE MOST IMPORTANT NETWORKS

While it is tempting to be influenced by the networking factors discussed previously, at the end of the day we fall into one of three networks:

- SM — Smart
- NS — Not Smart
- S   — Stupid

It's smart to network with others whom you can help and vice versa. It's not smart to let race, culture, gender, or *anything* other than genuine talent affect your decision. It's downright stupid to make a decision based on any of those factors before you meet someone.

If you discover that you are networking and not being success-ful, ask yourself if you are in a community of people who genuinely appreciate you for what you offer. Some are better than others.

Summary: Life is too short—don't waste your talents on people and communities that don't appreciate them.

17

Evil Networks

I was once asked if I was concerned people would "misuse" networking. Sadly it happens. A small group of tightly networked people caused September 11th. It's unlikely Bernie Madoff worked alone. Not all people contribute their skills to an honorable cause use. A friend from college had to extricate his daughter from a cult that had infiltrated her college dorm.

Summary: Any time we are asked to think or do something that we feel is wrong, it is time to evaluate the network and consider leaving it. Do not stay in an environment where you are asked to compromise your values.

18

Summary

My first car was a VW bug—with optional heat and no defrost. And those were the days before fleece. I had a bulky sleeping bag in the car that I would wrap around me so that I could have my shoulders covered and my feet out for the pedals. As I learned to master the clutch, I also discovered a muscle on the backside of my left leg that for the previous 20 years had gone completely undetected.

However, nothing was going to stop me from learning how to drive my new-to-me $800 magical machine.

Most of us clearly remember our nervous state of mind when we first learned to drive. Add to that the complications of a stick shift. Juggling our eagerness for freedom, the driving instructor's nerves, a few plastic cones, and a large parking lot, we were all set!

Clutch in, slowly pressing the accelerator—cough, cough!

What happened? We stalled.

As unbelievable as it may seem, we didn't get it right the first time. Even now, when there is some impatient person behind us in traffic, beeping to tell us how much he wants to be our new best friend, we sometimes rush, pop the car into gear, let out the clutch, and stall.

In due time, the percentage of successes began to far outpace the stalls. We were on our way to a new and exciting sense of freedom. Our newfound skill gave us confidence and a sense of adventure to explore the unknown.

Networking is similar. We need to be patient with ourselves. We didn't master all the moving parts of letting out the clutch, pressing the accelerator, and shifting the gears the very first time we tried it. The same was true with our first step.

Why do we expect to be proficient at networking? Unlike the situation with driving, where there are driver's education classes and state exams, we haven't had any training or education in networking.

Now let me ask you which is more important, the car or the gasoline? If you had to pick either hardware or software, what would you choose?

The questions are pointless. Why would you want a car without gasoline? Likewise, if you had great software, but no computer to use it with, what's the point?

The same is true with "hard skills" and "soft skills."

When I got the call to write this book, I calmly said, "Sure, no problem." Then I woke up and stared at the ceiling—what have I done? Next, I was on the phone calling people I knew and saying, "Would you be able to talk to me for a few minutes about a project?" Then I started meeting all kinds of new and fascinating people. Now close this book and make a call. Just say hello and ask what you can do for the person.

Happy networking!

Notes

CHAPTER 1

1. Autobiography of Benjamin Franklin, online; http://eserver.org/books/Franklin.
2. History of Rotary; RotaryHistory.org.

CHAPTER 2

1. *Merriam-Webster.*
2. Richard Boyle, *The Three Princes of Serendip*, 2000; http://livingheritage.org/three_princes.htm.
3. *Merriam-Webster.*
4. The Forum Corporation research quoted by Tom Peters.

CHAPTER 4

1. Nick Cafardo, "First Impressions," *Boston Globe*, August 17, 2002, p. E1.
2. Yale psychology professor Marianne LaFrance recently released "The Psychological Interpersonal and Social Effects of Bad Hair," www.nytimes.com/2001/05/026/nyregion/nyc-at-yale-a-discourse-on-hair.html?pagewanted=1.

3. Sheryl Lindsell-Roberts, *Business Writing for Dummies* (Foster City, Calif.: IDG Books Worldwide, Inc., 1999).
4. Richard C. Whiteley, *Love the Work You're With* (New York: Henry Holt, 2001), p. 157.

CHAPTER 6

1. Prof. Albert Mehrabian, "Decoding Inconsistent Communication," UCLA.
2. Beauty Before Age, San Francisco and Mill Valley; www.beauty beforeage.com.
3. Dotty LeMieux, "Here's the Wrinkle on Botox," *San Francisco Chronicle*, May 3, 2002.

CHAPTER 8

1. http://www.epromos.com/EducationCenter/messsendbooth .jhtml.

CHAPTER 10

1. Networking Survival Kit is a trademark of Effective Networking, Inc.
2. http://www.apa/org/journals/psp/psp791110.html.
3. http://www.fortune.com/indexw.jhtml?channel=artcol.jhtml& doc_id=209509.
4. From Meeting Planners International (MPI).
5. www.robertsrules.com.

CHAPTER 12

1. Dianne Durkin (president and founder of Loyalty Factor, LLC), interview with author.
2. Dana May Casperson, *Power Etiquette: What You Don't Know Can Kill Your Career* (New York: AMACOM, 1999).

CHAPTER 13

1. Jeff Taylor (founder of Monster.com), interview with author.
2. Malcolm Gladwell, *The Tipping Point* (New York: Back Bay Books, Little, Brown and Co., 2002).
3. Bob Metcalfe (founder of 3Com Corporation), interview with author.
4. Ted Koppel interview with David Letterman, July 9, 2002. For transcript, go to abcnews.go.com/sections/UpClose/DailyNews/upclose_letterman_transcript_020708.html.
5. Business for Social Responsibility; www.BSR.org.
6. Harley Owners Group; www.hog.org.

CHAPTER 14

1. Jeffrey Kluger, "Pumping Up Your Past," *Time*, June 10, 2002.
2. Dana May Casperson, *Power Etiquette: What You Don't Know Can Kill Your Career* (New York: AMACOM, 1999), p. 121.

CHAPTER 15

1. Exercises from Dr. Alison Domar, Harvard Mind Body Institute.
2. Vijai P. Sharma, *People-Fear, A Self-Help Book for Social Anxiety and Social Phobia* (Cleveland, Tenn.: Mind Publications, 1996), p. 12.

3. Ibid, p. 9.
4. Albert Einstein; http://www.brainyquote.com/quotes/quotes/a/albertein133991.html.

CHAPTER 16

1. http://www.nytimes.com/2009/10/04/magazine/04FOB-wwln-t.html?_r=2&scp=1&sq=gender%20gap&st=cse.
2. Anita Hill, "Insider Women with Outsider Values," *New York Times*, June 6, 2002.
3. http://movies.go.com/news/2001/8/gwynethfatsuit082101.html.

Bibliography

Alba, Jason. *I'm on LinkedIn—Now What??? A Guide to Getting the Most Out of LinkedIn,* 2nd ed. Cupertino, CA: Happy About, 2009.

Berent, Jonathan, and Amy Lemly. *Beyond Shyness: How to Conquer Social Anxieties.* New York: Simon & Schuster, 1993.

Bolles, Richard Nelson. *What Color Is Your Parachute? A Practical Manual for Job-Hunters and Career-Changers.* Berkeley, Calif.: Ten Speed Press, 2009.

Brooks, Donna, and Lynn Brooks. *Seven Secrets of Successful Women.* New York: McGraw-Hill, 1997.

Carnegie, Dale. *How to Win Friends and Influence People.* New York: Pocket Books, 1981.

Casperson, Dana May. *Power Etiquette: What You Don't Know Can Kill Your Career.* New York: AMACOM, 1999.

Covey, Stephen R. *The 7 Habits of Highly Effective People.* New York: Simon & Schuster, 1989.

Fitton, Laura, Michael Gruen, and Leslie Poston. *Twitters for Dummies.* Indianapolis, IN: Wiley Publishing, Inc., 2009.

Fox, Jeffrey J. *How to Become a Great Boss.* New York: Hyperion, 2002.

————. *How to Become a Rainmaker.* New York: Hyperion, 2000.

————. *How to Become CEO.* New York: Hyperion, 1998.

Gladwell, Malcolm. *The Tipping Point: How Little Things Can Make a Big Difference.* Boston: Little, Brown, 2002.

Goss, Tracy. *The Last Word on Power.* New York: Doubleday, 1996.

Gottesman, Deb, and Buzz Mauro. *The Interview Rehearsal Book: 7 Steps to Job-Winning Interviews Using Acting Skills You Never Knew You Had.* New York: Berkley Books, 1999.

Gray, John. *Mars and Venus in the Workplace.* New York: Harper-Collins, 2002.

————. *Men Are from Mars, Women Are from Venus.* New York: Harper-Collins, 1993.

Hagel, John, III, and Marc Singer. *Net Worth: Shaping Markets When Customers Make the Rules.* Boston: Harvard Business School Press, 1999.

Hinds, Karen S. *Get Along Get Ahead: 101 Courtesies for the New Workplace.* Boston: New Books Publishing, 2000.

Issacs, Florence. *Business Notes: Writing Personal Notes That Build Professional Relationships.* New York: Clarkson N. Potter/ Publishers, 1998.

Karen, Robert. "Shame." *Atlantic Monthly,* vol. 269, no. 2 (February 1992): 40–70.

Kipfer, Barbara Ann. *14,000 Things to Be Happy About.* New York: Workman Publishing, 1990.

Linver, Sandy. *Speak Easy: How to Talk Your Way to the Top.* New York: Summit Books, 1978.

————, and Jim Mengert. *Speak and Get Results.* New York: Fireside, 1994.

Lundun, Stephen C., et al. *Fish Tales.* New York: Hyperion, 2002.

Masciarelli, James P. *Power Skills: Building Top-Level Relationships for Bottom-Line Results.* Gloucester, MA: Nimbus Press, 2000.

McGinty, Sarah Myers. *Power Talk: Using Language to Build Authority and Influence.* New York: Warner Books, 2001.

Misner, Ivan R. *The World's Best Known Marketing Secret.* Austin, TX: Bard Press, 2000.

————, and Robert Davis. *Business by Referral: A Sure-Fire Way to Generate New Business.* Austin, TX: Bard Press, 1998.

————, and Don Morgan. *Masters of Networking.* Austin, TX: Bard Press, 2000.

Morgenstern, Julie. *Organizing from the Inside Out: The Foolproof System for Organizing Your Home, Your Office, and Your Life.* New York: Henry Holt, 1998.

Mundis, Jerrold. *Earn What You Deserve.* New York: Bantam Books, 1996.

Naisbitt, John. *Megatrends: Ten New Directions Transforming Our Lives.* New York: Warner Books, 1982.

Niven, David. *The 100 Simple Secrets of Happy People.* San Francisco: Harper, 2000.

Orman, Suze. *The Courage to Be Rich.* New York: Riverhead Books, 2002.

Pearlman, Leah; Carolyn Abrahm. *Facebook for Dummies.* Indianapolis, IN: Wiley Publishing, Inc., 2009.

Peck, Scott. *The Love You Deserve: 10 Keys to Perfect Love.* Solana Beach, CA: Lifepath Publishing, 1998.

Peters, Tom. *Reinventing Work: The Brand You 50.* New York: Borzoi, 1999.

————. *Reinventing Work: The Professional Service Firm 50.* New York: Borzoi, 1999.

————. *Reinventing Work: The Project 50*. New York: Borzoi, 1999.

Post, Peggy, and Peter Post. *The Etiquette Advantage in Business: Personal Skills for Professional Success*. New York: Harper Resource, 1999.

Ribbens, Geoff, and Richard Thompson. *Understanding Body Language*. Hong Kong: Barron's Educational Series, Inc., 2001.

Richardson, Cherryl. *Take Time for Your Life*. New York: Broadway Books, 1998.

RoAne, Susan. *The Secrets of Savvy Networking*. New York: Warner Books, 1993.

Sandler, David H. *You Can't Teach a Kid to Ride a Bike at a Seminar*. Stevenson, MD: Bayhead Publishing, Inc., 1999.

Schenkel, Susan. *Giving Away Success: Why Women Get Stuck and What to Do about It*. New York: Harper Perennial, 1991.

Schmidt, Peggy J. *Making It on Your First Job: When You're Young, Inexperienced and Ambitious*. New York: Avon Books, 1981.

Seligman, Martin E. P. *Learned Optimism*. New York: Pocket Books, 1998.

Sinetar, Marsha. *Do What You Love, the Money Will Follow: Discovering Your Right Livelihood*. New York: Dell Publishing, 1987.

Stanley, Thomas J. *Networking with the Affluent and Their Advisors*. New York: McGraw-Hill, 1993.

Stanny, Barbara. *Prince Charming Isn't Coming: How Women Get Smart about Money*. New York: Viking, 1997.

Stephens, Nancy J., and Bob Adams. *Customer Focused Selling*. Holbrook, Mass.: Adams Media Corporation, 1998.

Tillquist, Kristin. *Capitalizing on Kindness: Why 21st Century Professionals Need to Be Nice.* Franklin Lakes, NJ: Career Press, 2009.

Weber, Larry. *The Provocateur.* New York: Crown Business, 2001.

Whiteley, Richard C. *Love the Work You're With.* New York: Henry Holt, 2001.

Index

About the Author

Diane Darling considers herself a friendly, functional introvert. While she is adept at being at a cocktail party, she doesn't look forward to it. She developed her skills as a child by living in several countries and by just being curious. She prefers to network through writing, being a speaker, and by connecting people.

Most recently she was the keynote speaker at MIT Charm School. She has worked with a variety of corporations, nonprofits, universities, and government agencies. She has been featured on NBC *Nightly News*, in the *Wall Street Journal, Washington Post, San Francisco Chronicle, International Herald Tribune* just to name a few. She is based in Boston, MA.

CPSIA information can be obtained at www.ICGtesting.com
Printed in the USA
LVOW12s1017070814

397886LV00013B/416/P